Help! I'm Not Me

By

David Berthelot

Carol Royce

2010

Grosvenor House
Publishing Limited

This book is based on an original manuscript written by David Berthelot
between 2001 and 2005.

Some names and identifying criteria have been changed to protect
the privacy of individuals.

All biographical details, personal comments, and information offered by
Carol Royce are as supplied by her, and the author does not accept any legal
responsibility if these are incomplete, inaccurate, or out of date.

David Berthelot is hereby identified as author of this
work in accordance with Section 77 of the Copyright, Designs
and Patents Act 1988

The book cover picture is copyright to David Berthelot
Front cover image - David Berthelot
Back cover image - Peter Berthelot

This book is published by
Grosvenor House Publishing Ltd
Link House
140 The Broadway, Tolworth, Surrey, KT6 7HT.
www.grosvenorhousepublishing.co.uk

A CIP record for this book
is available from the British Library

ISBN 978-1-908105-43-1

Preface by David Berthelot

For most of my life I have been interested in helping people. I met Carol Royce through her being a friend of my father and mother, Peter and Diane. Eventually she asked me to write her biography. 'Help! I'm not me' describes Carol's effort to overcome gender dysphoria while showing how important it is to value the uniqueness of every human being.

Knowledge I gained during my philosophical studies at the University of East Anglia and on counselling skills training courses, along with my work supporting and teaching vulnerable adults, reinforced my interest in behaviour and experience. It encouraged me to consider both more thoughtfully. Furthermore, a desire to increase my understanding of the human condition had already led me on a complicated yet fascinating journey. Consequently, it felt right to accept the challenge of working on this project so in 2001 I did. It was not long before I was bogged down with a mass of detail that took literally years to sort. My frustration at trying to convert all the information Carol was eagerly presenting into something readable often interfered with the flow of the writing process. Not wanting to dampen her enthusiasm I gave her the freedom to be herself. It was always my intention that she told her own story. For the purpose of clarification some of my reflections have been integrated into her account and occasional commentary from me printed in italics.

Acknowledgement by David Berthelot

I would like to thank my father and mother Peter and Diane Berthelot for their kindness and encouragement to complete this book.

Introduction by Carol Royce

What do you do when you know you are different in a manner that causes problems? You want to fit in with society, but your body shape, a birthmark, some line or spot on your face, how you look by the way you walk, talk and do everyday things, stands out. The details about you that stand out are generally seen as weird, awkward and not the norm, leading many to think that at best you are something to be pitied, at worst a freak to be avoided or got rid of.

I had always felt uncomfortable with my male body. Before becoming my true self I was labelled 'gender dysphoric' or 'transsexual'. Transsexuals are people, male or female, who are convinced they are trapped in the wrong sex. I hate the word 'transsexual'. For me, it is an ugly, male expression that sounds like a juggernaut rolling across the Australian outback. I prefer 'gender dysphoric' which is the psychiatrists' term for my former condition. 'Trans man' or 'Trans woman', 'transgender' and 'Trans person' are likewise used to describe it - all better than 'transsexual'.[1][2][3]

As a sufferer of gender dysphoria, I lived its contradictions. I was born male. At least, that is what the delivery team who helped bring me into the world decided. Looking back, I believe I knew as early as three or four years old there was something wrong with me. Unhappiness followed, made worse by the grief I got from others. Although there were positive influences around me such as my family, fate worked against me, moulding me into an angry young person. I was on a setting to self-destruct.

Transsexuals are still not seen objectively by many of the rule makers and judges of human behaviour in our culture who have power over us. Literally adding insult to injury, moralists - including some with particularly strong opinions - neighbours, and so-called friends, won't listen.

I am telling the story of my search for my real self hoping it will help the similarly challenged. To begin with I wouldn't admit who I was in those dark, early days: this confused individual swinging between doubt and certainty. At a conscious level, I was hiding from what I saw then as the social stigma that went with my quandary. I disliked being different and passed myself off as somebody else to make everyone happy. Cracks began to show. To survive, I destroyed the love of those closest to me, my better half and kids most of all. I was deceitful. I didn't care about anyone but myself. A lot of what I did was selfish and irresponsible. It reached a stage where my one and only goal was to be female and anything that blocked this was kicked to one side.

The thought of hurting people - particularly my partner and children - shocks me. If there is one overarching truth this story highlights, it is how easy it was for me to mess up my life and my family's as well. With David's help I want to explain why I lived this way.

I expect many of you will find my experiences hard to understand. They are here inside me now and always will be; they will never leave me. I want to share these so you may appreciate what I failed to when I was going through them.

Those who are unhappy about their biological gender should know they can see a doctor if they need to who will arrange an appointment for them to attend a gender clinic. It is important that when a person's difference from others could lead them to be rejected they are at least treated with compassion and if possible empathy. They are still unique and valid human beings with potential.[4]

Notes

1 The prefix *trans* can mean across, over, beyond, above, moving, and changing. For me, transgender is a person's gender identity in a state of flux. Trans man, Trans woman, Trans person and Trans people at least hint at transsexuals being more human and acceptable than they are often portrayed. I cannot say I like these terms a lot, but I was more comfortable being called a Trans woman than a transsexual; all imply that someone is between one state and another. Of course, I am no longer in this position. I *am* a woman.

2 An umbrella term for gender dysphoria is gender identity disorder.

3 Transgender individuals feel their assigned gender role at birth and the resulting expectations society has of them do not fit their own internal sense of self; they are deeply troubled by and urged to dispel this conflict.

4 There are also those who do not agree that categorising individuals as either male or female is a necessary condition of personal identity, and actually claim to live their lives gender free.[i] I cannot see how anyone totally escapes being moulded to fit into our society's bi-polarised gender system. Surely there has to be a gendered society to help us make sense of our lives? It is hard to imagine survival of the human species without that starting point of the differences between males and females shaping and guiding behaviour to form the bases for the development of individual social identities.

i Christie, Elan Cane, The Fallacy of the Myth of Gender, Gendys Conference, USA and London, 2000.

Chapter One

Flashing lights on ambulances, fire engines and police cars became part of the chaos. Their sirens sounded together like a bad orchestra gatecrashing my thoughts. I wasn't sure whether the strobing was coming from the emergency vehicles or I had started hallucinating. My instinct was to help control the blaze, but in my semi-conscious state the visual disturbances and noise added to my confusion.

I was running a business refurbishing service stations across the country. One of my responsibilities in this role was to supervise cleaning out the petrol tanks. I often had to go inside them to check they had been done properly. On that defining day in 1984 I was inspecting one at a garage in Pin Green, Hertfordshire. Some feet below, in a dark, claustrophobic space, I was talking to one of my men. He was on the surface standing above me watching the manhole through which I had entered. When my employee accidentally kicked a Stillson wrench[1] down it, hitting the strike plate, sparks shot off this structure that was welded to the floor. An explosion knocked him over. There was one vivid flash and extreme heat, a massive rush of air propelling me upward triggering a chain reaction, vapour residues in the other tanks also igniting.[2] I staggered forward, going through the motions of my usual "I can cope with it" attitude. Aware of the smell of my flesh and hair burning, I collapsed. One witness reported that I looked as if a polythene bag had melted onto my face. It was like I had stepped out of reality into a world operating in slow motion.

On my arrival at Billericay hospital, staff had to cut off what remained of my clothes.

Every movement was sore. My assurance I was female competing with the brute fact I had a male body was made worse by this new debacle. Inside, I was screaming for release from years of false promises and misuse. The ugly signs of my physical injuries beginning to heal could easily have stood for the slowly resolving clash of emotions within me. I joked that pig skin was laid over the damaged areas to encourage my own to grow again.

I had to spend about eight weeks in hospital doing very little. This gave me the chance to think. Realising I had been close to death, I asked myself why in the past I had no concern for my own safety. Used to doing dangerous things like drinking and driving over the speed limit, it never occurred to me that if I didn't learn to curb these impulses I could end up being responsible for someone's death. In that ward I saw how I had squandered many opportunities to show some integrity.

There had to be a better way for me to live. I was thirty-three. Enlightenment brought me to the conclusion that I had wasted the majority of those years and offended many people along the way. The person I hurt the most was my partner, Jackie.

Remembering the sight and sound of my infant daughter Sophie crying when I tried to pick her up and cuddle her while I was still in pain and wearing the dressings upsets me even today. The poor state I was in meant that temporarily the physical and psychological pressure on me was greater than my ability to cope.

Before the accident I found it easy to make money. I had a generous income that wasn't damaged by the recession gripping the country. Although I ran a successful business, primarily to finance my life, it was a long way from the cosy suburbia many appeared happy with. Paying the household expenses, including the food costs and the children's clothes bill, proved I could act responsibly, but most of the money went on 'the perversion', as Jackie called it. By continuing to support my family I had a clearer conscience. Me, my partner, and others who had a strong influence on my rationale, played the pretend game; I shammed it into my forties.

I used the male role to camouflage my female sentience. This persisted until 1993 when I managed to find help. In 1984, at the moment of the blast, I was partially shaken free of my unreal self which made me aware of who I had to be. My mind said: "Stop this. Be you."

You have to accept and explore your real inner self to be genuine: you cannot spend a lifetime pretending without trouble somewhere along the line.

Recovery in hospital and later at home was spent getting rid of an arrogant ego that you might think of as a snake shedding its outer skin.

Having survived the ordeal, perhaps hardened and tempered by it, during convalescence the shocking reality of my true gender identity hit me.

My struggle began in the womb. By all appearances, I was born a male in Central Middlesex Hospital, Park Royal, near Greenford, at 7.45 a.m. on 2nd November, 1950. What lay ahead were catastrophes of love, money, violence, and probably the deepest despair the human psyche could stand.

Notes

1 A Stillson wrench is a large, heavy, adjustable spanner otherwise known as a monkey wrench.
2 Immediately before the blast, my position inside the tank was standing on the bottom directly beneath the manhole above at the foot of a ladder connecting to the surface.

Chapter Two

In some ways, my life was like that of any kid who grew up in the fifties. My mum and dad didn't have much, but they coped. Dad earned very little. Mum looked after my twin brother and I. It was hard for them both as dad was in the army. We used to share with my maternal grandmother. Friction was common in the cramped conditions we lived in, nan something else where mum was concerned. They were always arguing. Nan seemed to pick on mum a lot. Even at that stage, my problem was coming out in my behaviour. Being so young, I didn't know how to deal with it.

I used to like visiting the canal near nan's house. It ran behind the whole length of the Bath works, including the Aladdin light bulb factory, spanning many miles to Greenford station and beyond.

My Auntie Pat initially supervised my brother and I on rambles. She was always taking us for walks. We found our own routes which began the same as hers then changed course as our built-in radar picked up and led us to whatever trouble there was in the vicinity.

On my own by the canal I used to think about jumping in, then I thought: "I can't do it; it's filthy." It was as well. I saw dead fish floating on the surface. Placed behind an iron foundry that was a plant during the war where nan played her version of Russian roulette working with munitions, over the years this artificial waterway was sullied by a toxic melting pot and should have had warning signs with skulls and crossbones painted on them deposited at regular intervals along the bank. A conduit for the factories close-by, in a former epoch barges drifted down it carrying the coal that fed these sweatshops.

Folk often talk about how close they were to their grandparents. I remember my granddad Simmons with particular fondness and how once while sitting on his knee he offered me simple, much needed words of comfort in a volatile household.

"Everything will be all right," he said to me, shortly before he died.

It was as if he knew something about me others didn't. I used to carry the large tin of Hack cough sweets we both liked over to him. He would give me one, take another for himself, and together we would enjoy that hot, menthol flavour bomb. I think granddad was addicted to them. From what I have been told, he nearly turned me into a Hack addict.

Granddad Simmons died about the year 1955. Nan Simmons lived to an advanced age. One of eight children, the youngest of whom was actually her half-brother - the result of a brief flirt nan had taking her bartering instinct too far - mum knew what it meant to be part of an unconventional tribe. Using me as a runner, frequently sending me off to the old corner shop to swap eggs from the chickens she kept that were often pecking round her house and garden and sitting on her dining room table or in her pantry, nan was a mistress of survival through exchanging goods and services. In today's EU climate her poor hygiene would have had her put away as a danger to public health. Whenever she was cooking she would lean over the stove with a fag in her mouth that was more ash than cigarette.

I remember mum reflecting on what a shameless community the stomping ground of her youth looked. She recalled how one day she came home with her latest boyfriend and the first thing they saw as they walked through the garden was a condom like a windsock hanging from a neighbour's washing line. Mum said she grinned with the awkwardness of an embarrassed virgin. Washable condoms were manufactured in this country circa 1930 to 1940. This led me to think that if around 1940 foreign spies spotted these large sheaths on British washing lines, they might imagine our boys were all well-hung and could form macho warrior armies strong enough to win the war.

Sentimentalising about the Simmons clan temporarily brought me forward several years to brood on an episode I would rather forget. Practically everyone except me knew my uncle Pete, whom I adored, was ill. Nobody bothered to tell me and because I was so hurt by that I have not seen certain members of my family since. When Pete died in 1995 he was one of the few people I cried for. Breaking down at his funeral, I realised there were events for which I couldn't keep up the impression I was tough.

Both in their early twenties, mum and dad began their journey of adult responsibility in the prime of their youth. They lived in Germany when my brother Michael and I were still quite young, first in Düsseldorf then later Hamburg. Around 1956, after serving in Malaya for a while, dad left the army and the family found itself entering a new phase.

From the age of four, I started to struggle to keep up this image of boyhood. Somehow it began to feel uncomfortable, like I was left-handed but having to use my right. Michael, who was fifteen minutes older than me, seemed comfortable being a boy. Although we were twins I don't think Michael and I were much alike. I would even go as far as to say we were total opposites.

When I was seven we got our place in Harlow. It was exciting moving from London to what was then the country with all that open space.

The house we moved into was new. Mum and dad still live there. It was on a small estate surrounded by fields. Sadly, most of the original green area was swallowed and digested by the London overspill. The playing fields and allotments behind them remain, just. From all other angles they are faced with an ever-increasing sprawl of concrete and cars. Now the manor has turned into a giant car park where finding a parking space is a common cause of dispute.

During childhood the place was ideal for me. I would cut across these little streams in my Wellington boots, in a sense, I suppose, finding my way in the world. Walking through Epping Forest was pure freedom. My private adventures were untouched by fear. Time meant nothing to me in my universe of innocent dreams. Once I became aware of it again I had to step out of my realm and go home. I was sad to leave. Being on my own lifted the pressure a little. Out there I didn't have to prove myself to anyone. As soon as I got back to base I had to slot into this role I hated. My return was usually met by the words: "Where the hell have you been?" from mum. I would be rude to her, get a slap for it, then be sent to bed.

Being locked in my room was not an effective punishment. The meadows were rich with species and it was from these origins I found my acting soulmate. A rectangle of cardboard under my bed was refuge for a friend I valued almost as much as my solitude. To me he looked like a grass snake. He would curl up on my bed, eyeballing me adoringly, showing me his sliver of a tongue darting in and out of his mouth, tasting the air. Occasionally, he would lie on my stomach. When he got curious he might go for a slither. Reliable to the end, he always came back to me and the comfort of his shoe box.

Several months after I extracted him, during a nature lesson at school our teacher asked us whether we had any unusual pets. By that he meant ferrets, rats, etcetera, not the type of creature found in my possession. I had something that ate them. Putting my hand up I told our class that I had a grass snake and a feeling of extreme pride flushed through me when I was asked by our teacher to bring it to school.

Armed with the shoe box - an apt phrase as it turned out - the next day I brought my charge to show the class. Our teacher slowly removed the lid of my makeshift container then with a look of deep concern on his face peered inside. Moby showed his head. To me, he was being friendly, that tongue of his going full throttle. A hush pervaded the room through our teacher's shock at the nestling shape he discerned. Moby popped his kisser through a useful gap. Our teacher broke the silence: "This isn't a grass snake. It's an adder." Having thought how cute my reptilian buddy was with his distinctive markings it did occur to me that he looked different from the standard specimens I had seen. Desperately pushing the lid of the box back down, Sir secured and removed it from the classroom. He then arranged for the RSPCA to come and pick it up. As far as I know, Moby spent the rest of his days in the reptile house at the kiddies' pets' corner zoo in Harlow Park. The entire period I had him he seldom appeared nervous in my company or showed any hostility towards me. Adders are venomous snakes, yet

I was never bitten by Moby. As I was the provider of his food and housing maybe he let me off? I thought that, like me, he was unusual, and probably why in my naive, childish mind I saw us both as kindred spirits.

If I wasn't kept indoors by mum and dad I would be off again the next day, stay out for hours and be late back. Lying to mum over where I had been became a regular occurrence. To avoid punishment I would tell her I was at a friend's address.

Although I tried not to show it my attitude was one of contempt for everyone except those I cared about. Mum having two more boys didn't help and as time passed I vented my anger on all three of my brothers. Out walking, deep in my reverie, I used to think: "How dare my mum have more boys. I want a sister."

It is easy to assume the female sibling I coveted would have been someone I trusted in. An understanding sister might have helped me. In all honesty, I was frustrated I couldn't tell mum and dad how I felt. I remember looking at mum thinking: "If anyone should know what's wrong with me, it's you."

I hid the real me. On the outside I was a little boy. Public enemy misread the signals I gave off, which were already wrong. I wanted to be seen as tough and streetwise. They saw me as this nasty, aggressive kid. I had to show them I could play normal. This caused me to suppress the little girl, whom I believed to be my real inner self. She wouldn't be silenced and this complicated my life. I was an incomplete jigsaw the remaining pieces of which I couldn't find anywhere.

My dad would put boxing gloves on my twin brother and I and spar with us on the lawn in the back garden. He would clobber me probably because I was being a tad rough, and it hurt. I'd take it but I'd cry on the qt. Revealing sensitivity implied weakness; I didn't show my softer emotions. I was totally back to front, always the tough bit before the soft. Mixed up and unable to talk to mum and dad about it, whatever *it* was, the tension within me continued to build.

Now I appreciate that mum was having problems of her own. Having four sprogs all demanding her attention made her ill. In those days depression wasn't dealt with properly. Currently it is recognised as a genuine illness and there is less stigma attached to it. Poor mum had to knuckle down. I remember thinking how resilient she was.

Mum and I are both calmer than we were. Back then it took a lot to make us angry. Like her, if anybody pushed me too far I'd explode. No matter who was on the receiving end of it I'd have to let my anger out, then it would be over.

Existence got better for mum. As a child you don't understand what is happening to your parents, failing to comprehend their struggle keeping the daily routine together. Quoting her almost verbatim, mum told me: "Once the kids start growing up you get out of that cloud and appreciate your family." Mum and dad are still there for us.

Although I believed I should try to be otherwise, it felt right for me to go my way and that included playing with dolls. I loved the idea of dressing up. Often I would hang around mum's legs watching her put her make-up on. For me that was natural.

To the world I was a boy. Mum dressed me in boys' clothes. I would take them all off and walk about in my underpants. Outside, picking up a toy car rather than my preferred object was part of the act. Inside I was saying: "I wish I could play with dolls."

Michael adopted all my stuff. He would happily lie on the sitting room floor at home with the soldiers, forts and whatnots belonging to us, while I'd be out on my own exploring. If I dabbled with boys' toys it would be because I liked the dudes in the playground and the only way I could interact with them was to have a prop to hand like a Dinky truck. Unless I wanted the perfect reason for being off school for two months I knew I couldn't steam into a group of lads with a dolly.

As for Michael, he was just there. I don't mean that unkindly.

I was his protector. When he was around me I looked out for him. Cliché or not, it's true that without a word passing between us I almost always knew if he was in trouble. I spent a large part of my childhood helping him overcome some sort of hurdle or another.

Life is often a lot of hassle for a little happiness. I have lived it and although the events I am focusing on are in the past, they feel so present.

People were always picking on Michael because he was quiet. The bullies of the school used to zoom in on him as if he wore a bright orange t-shirt with "Victim - walk all over me please" printed across it.

It was the school Mafia: the hit men, who were cowards in disguise, feeding off the weak and vulnerable. The bullies' self-esteem was probably quite low too until they had done over a few underdogs. I was the kamikaze deliverer of justice on a death mission, carrying the handkerchief with the red dot on it.

Don't get me wrong. Michael wasn't weak. He was sensitive: he would handle strife his own subdued way which was all right for him. I would have to jump in and take control. Any time I bailed him out of a scrape he would say: "What did you do that for?" meaning: "Why did you interfere? I was dealing with it."

On leaving school, Michael became a butcher, coming home from work every day stinking of meat. His emigration to Australia was an impressive leap of independence that was to be snatched away from him almost as soon as he got there. Called up by the Australian government to do military service, while traipsing through a jungle he was hit by a stray bullet that shattered one of his kneecaps. Bleeding profusely, the exposed wound made contact with the dense, suffocating hell that whispered promises of death to my brother as he fought to remain conscious. That absurd, deranged crusade known as the Vietnam War eating away his spirit made him a hero of his family through being wounded in action and invalided out of the army, surviving what, like in any stupid, pointless conflict, many on both sides didn't. Imagining that before the incident he spontaneously recalled a top chart song amid tropical forest mixing uneasily with oppressive humidity and cruelness, it struck me how ridiculous popular culture is against a background of violence, injury, and death. Visions of helicopters, their staccato noise disturbing the last traces of peace left in him as he hoped to arrest the savagery of the human condition, told me how fortunate I was not to have been there.

Michael still lives in Australia. Despite his injury he can count himself lucky he got home and had a life afterwards. I hear he is doing all right.

Allen is mum and dad's third child: 'the middle one' as he is called. Always a big lad, you might say he was built for his destiny. I wouldn't have thought it possible for mum to have a baby the size he was at birth. He weighed more than ten pounds. Before falling pregnant with him mum was about eight stone. While he grew in her womb mum's dimensions were seriously stretched. He nearly split her sides. That wasn't the 'funny ha-ha' meaning of that phrase either, for I can't imagine mum would have rated it a joke when she was in labour with him. Looking three months old when he was born, my brother's physical development was rapid. You couldn't pick him up easily when he was a toddler and if you did manage to you soon put him down.

Having another male child in the house unsettled me. It felt like he was intruding on my territory. I spent most of his early years trying to sell him to anyone who called at the front door.

Allen is still big. He is twice my width and a lot taller. From leaving school he went into the army, the REME, a section that drove great transporters around to pick up damaged vehicles, including armoured cars, low loaders and trucks, for repair. I have been told he and some of his mates nearly wiped out part of a German village while taking a tank for a spin when they were all drunk. Ignoring the health and safety concerns of everyone in the area, they supposedly drove through a housing estate. How reliable was Allen's memory of the alleged incident?

The story was told at family reunions and pub crawls, either by the man himself or one of his mates. From their perspective I was another bloke whom they accepted into their unofficial drinking club. I would put up with listening to this tale several times over the years, as I did most of their incredible stories. Cringing at their male bragging, I would appear interested, then retreat into myself. They were like cartoon characters living in a virtual world; I saw many things as caricatures. I tried to understand this stereotypically masculine place by stepping out of my dimension into theirs and I didn't fit.

If I had gone into the army I would never have hacked it because I was too self-centred. Although I accept that women can enrol and express what I arguably call a macho side to their femaleness, I have always viewed the defence services - particularly the army - as essentially male in character and therefore largely if not wholly at odds with the finer details of femininity as I understand them. There was no future for me at an institution that went in an opposing direction. Facing enlistment - or in the event of a world war, conscription - I would still not have fitted in such an establishment. Back then I couldn't be told anything. I thought I knew it all. In this sense dad was the same as me at that age. He also believed he knew everything there was to know about life. Unlike me, he was able to adapt to the army regime and loved it.

I accept that discipline is necessary for those who, with some knocking into shape, fit that lifestyle. Had I followed the pattern of my brothers and joined up I would have been stifled because my superiors were trying to mould me into something far removed from my real self. I have put up with being denied or losing much of my freedom to be me without going near the army. It does help many people to make sense of the world though, offering them intensive physical activity with structure and purpose.

I have a lot of affection for Terry who is the youngest member of our family. One moment he was a baby, the next he had left school.

Certainly I remember having to look after him. Ideas flashed through my mind as I pushed him along the road in his pram: that excuse for a vehicle - one of those big, bouncy jobs with the large springs - is branded on my memory. Terry wanted to hang on to an easy life for as long as he could. It was convenient for him to put off learning to walk.

Despite the fact there was a ten year age gap between us, Terry and I were close. Under my supervision he nearly left his pram in spirit. I tried to float it across a pond with him inside. It sank more or less immediately. The hullabaloo of a gush of panicking adults running from the community centre across the cycle track to the water's edge was one of the best laughs I have had. In those first confusing seconds the more practical staff members of a nearby children's play activities scheme tried to find out exactly what had happened. The leader was looking for facts that amounted to my nautical error. What I had done out of curiosity, or, more accurately, stupidity, was an experiment doomed to failure. The first priority was to fish the pram out. I have introduced all my brothers to things that could have killed them and should be ashamed of myself but I'm not. Childcare was not my forté. I found it a burden. As an exercise the pram stunt seemed like a good idea, not from the point of view of seeing if Terry survived it, but to find out what we could do. I called myself a genius while everyone else dubbed me idiotic. Had the thingamajig floated, with my mentality I would have got in it with him and sailed around until I was bored.

What was rescued, apart from Terry, his cherubic face beaming with smiles, was a messy, gunged up heap of salvage which at that stage failed as a pram. The contraption, all covered in mud, was back to a kind of normal. Before it went in the drink its rubber wheels looked brilliant white. Thereafter they were permanently stained grey. Mum still has what I call a misplaced affection for it even though she sold it as soon as she could.

Terry has forgiven me for nearly drowning him as a baby. Mum and I often laugh over the sinking pram affair. Since everything has been brought out in the open we have got on better. When Terry is here he lightens my mood, inspiring fresh vistas of opportunity. He is a lovely man and always calls me his big sister. I find him understanding. Without fail, he values and respects me.

On saying I wasn't cut out for childcare, I knew on the surface that was a joke linked to my childhood experience looking after Terry. I have never had maternal feelings. In the role of adult male I had children with both spouses. It wasn't me who nurtured them. My consorts brought them up while I followed my selfish lifestyle. When ours came along I loved them. They weren't planned. Had entitlement to the luxury of gender realignment come earlier I would have preferred to have been a career woman with a partner - no children. Now I am in a position to say I still haven't any maternal feelings and that is after hormone therapy and gender realignment surgery. I get on well with my brothers' and friends' offspring. It is no secret I like them; I always want to hand them back when their parents are ready to take them home.

We already know how annoying I could be when I was a kid. I am sure there were times when my mum and dad wished they could have given me to someone else.

Intrigued by Carol's description of her childhood I wanted to know how she managed the contradiction between her inner female self and her male persona under stress.

I remember an incident that happened when I was about fourteen concerning someone who upset Michael. It was one of those situations where it felt as if a torrent of aggressive energy came from me in the form of a short, powerful discharge of anger like a blast of steam escaping from a pipe. This boy pushed Michael while we were messing around in the cricket pavilion near our home. He didn't want Michael to have a say in what we should do. I got him in a headlock which he soon found his way out of. We had a fist fight that amounted to punching the air with some evasive action thrown in: it looked more like we were dancing and I wondered if our feminine sides were coming out in protest at the stupidity of it all. Spotting his chance, he made for the big old tree that stood in the middle of the field where we used to play regularly. He managed to scale it, failing to anticipate my determination to get him. I caught hold of one of his legs and yanked it, pulling him from the branches. Next moment, he was lying on the ground. I had broken his arm. That kid eventually got over his clash with me, and Michael never had any harassment from him again. Mixing with boys in the school playground, in my street, and wherever else, frequently sparked my aggressive side. Amid these spells of unease the emotion would burst out of me. There would always be a reason for this happening. I didn't look for trouble. Perhaps it was an important part of my process of becoming?

Being able to deal with my anger in the right way only came through learning self-discipline. As a child, I didn't have any. Later, having made many mistakes, I realised I couldn't get far without considering other people's feelings and points of view.

During a recent visit home I noticed the ancient oak had been cut down. It must have been centuries old. Those responsible have taken away a piece of my childhood. I think several fellow juveniles and probably those of generations before us had climbed up and added their names to that tree. By leaving the signs of our youth on it did we contribute to its death? Over the years, could all those kids gouging the bark, which was its protective layer, not only have interfered with an organic way of being but also shortened a life? I would like to believe it died naturally. Our own lives are a privilege allowed us by nature and it could end them at any moment.

This made me think of why we should respect natural laws.

Another feat of stupidity I was responsible for that involved Michael began with us and some local lads meeting on a playing field to try out a bow and arrow he had made. Michael was reluctant to let anyone else touch his creation, let alone have a go of it, so I snatched it from him. I prepared the arrow for firing. As I pulled the bow back, my self-control went AWOL. Aiming the weapon directly at Michael, I fired the arrow. It split the air with the sound of a whip cracking, hitting Michael on the forehead. The tip pierced his skin, drawing blood. His cries must have alerted the whole of Harlow. It felt like parts of London would have heard them as well. He still carries the scars of the event.

Once I vented my anger I'd be still for a while then the tension would start building up inside me again until the next explosive release which could be weeks later or the next day. My single-mindedness didn't help. If I wanted to do something I would do it. I couldn't have cared less about the consequences. I have always demanded justice. I was aware of these two forces inside me competing with each other, one I wanted there, one I didn't.

Being reckless was my way of experimenting. One year - I was about ten - I decided to find out what would happen if I put a match to the Christmas decorations. Pleading with me not to do it, Michael, whose well-developed common sense could have saved our family a lot of nuisance if circumstances had gone his way, found himself witness to my act of vandalism. I struck a match then held it against one of the paper doodahs which soon caught. Flames rolled across the ceiling. Streamers going from the four corners of the living room to the middle with bells and other seasonal shapes filling the gaps provided the fuel and course for their trail. Thirty seconds was all it took to wipe out those Yuletide knick-knacks. Michael and I managed to stop the fire while dicing with injury. By the time mum and dad returned we had cleared the worst of the debris. When dad saw a black ceiling with no decorations, out of the first hell I had created another was let loose.

Eventually dad calmed down. He grounded us both for days. No punishment or restriction stopped me from following my instincts and acting on impulse. At secondary school, nicking this boy's bike because I had to have it was all part of an ordinary day for me. Having no conscience over stealing it, I kept the cycle for several weeks before throwing it in the local pond. I befriended the boy who owned it, having the front to salvage it from its temporary resting place then receive a reward from his dad for my trouble. Mum remembers this. It was behaviour typical of me.

Deliberating over the controversy I created, I wonder how I ever made it through childhood without being put away. That drive to go out into the world and get what I wanted caused me to form a protective bubble around myself that was to remain for a large part of my life.

Chapter Three

Many girls in their teens would become hysterical if they noticed the slightest bodily change that caused them to feel unattractive. As for the odd attack of acne this could be a matter of life and death because the pimply skin disease threatens to leave permanent scars on their faces. These features are the downside of growing up. I certainly didn't slot comfortably into my teens. I suppose I was about twelve when confusion really hit me.

Today I can look back and say most of the things that interested boys bored me. Several of the lads in my class thought being in the school football team was the business. If I had been picked for it I would have found a way to get out of playing.

During the summer of 1963 dad took us all to London to visit his sister Midge and mum's brother Pete who were married to each other and lived in Camberwell. Exploring these new surroundings was my one and only mission then and I had to do it on my own. I remember walking for ages, gobsmacked by all the red buses that kept coming because it seemed as though there were about three a day in Harlow, the place was so small.

Reaching the depot at Camberwell Green, I discovered a park on the opposite side of the road and decided to sit on a bench there watching these monsters go by. A young lad, his face covered in acne, plonked himself down beside me. This boy was to have a dramatic effect on my life.

About five minutes went by before he started talking while furiously writing down details of the buses in a book. Route numbers appeared on the front of these symbols of London public transport - huge metal mammoths lumbering their way along the cluttered streets of the city suburbs. Shouting data at me as if I was a collector of such trivia and knew the destinations before I said a word to him, this boy set the pace. He forged the link between us on his terms. The first thing I had to do was enjoy his hobby. He fathomed which of the vehicles were late and which of them were punctual. I wasn't interested. He looked at me and said: "My name's Steve. What's yours?"

Perhaps it was then I should have got up and walked away.

"Never talk to strangers," my mum and dad kept telling us. I thought strangers were always adults; I never imagined they could be around my age.

The boy had this refreshing liveliness that made him stand out. He spoke quickly, sometimes in an abrupt way.

"Have you been to Tower Bridge?" he enquired and after I said "No" I had to ask him if it mattered what my name was. In the chaotic crossfire of words he came straight back with: "Course it don't."

His acceptance of me and his respect for my right to anonymity made me feel comfortable with him. There didn't appear to be any way to stop him talking though. It was defensive, impatient, insecure, discursive prattling that suggested to me he didn't want to answer any questions I might ask. Throughout my life I have met a lot of people like this.

Steve couldn't bear silence. He had to fill it. His favourite words were some that up until then I had never heard of. Sod was the worst I had come across. Saying that in front of the folks would have got me curfewed for a week. Others he used were dink and spamhead. He was talking a whole new language called streetwise.

When I did manage to get a word into a space missed by Steve I asked him where he resided.

"Where I want," came his sharply concise answer.

"How?" I pressed. I was so green I thought everyone around my age lived at home.

"I just do, right?" he blustered.

Inspired by Steve's resourcefulness at what would then have been about fourteen years old, I wanted to be part of his campaign against adult control. I was answerable to my mum and dad. Here was a guy who at fourteen had cracked the dependency on parents problem. He hung out where he liked. No one bossed him around. I told him my abode was in Harlow and thought I'd blown my chances of joining him.

"Where's 'arlow?" he blasted at me.

I left him sitting on the bench having promised Auntie Midge I would rejoin our family group for tea at five o'clock. He advised I meet him at the same place around a similar time the following day. Still having a conversation with him as I walked off, I shouted that I had to return to Essex that night with my mum and dad. He yelled: "I'll be here."

On my return to Midge and Pete's I begged mum to allow me to stay longer as we were on holiday from school. Pete promised he would make sure I caught the right bus home on Sunday which was a Green Line from Aldgate station. That was the first of my many visits to London.

Excitement at the thought of seeing Steve again drove me back to that park bench almost twenty-four hours later. Already there, Steve looked at me saying: "I knew you'd come."

"How did you know?" I queried.

"I just did," came the reply.

Immediately, I was catapulted into his dangerous world. Loath to take a breath except to stop him from collapsing through lack of oxygen - although he was probably more in danger of hyperventilating - Steve treated me as if we had known each other for years. We had been sitting there for about an hour when he suggested we had something to eat.

"There's a café down by the kiosk," he said. The kiosk was a small lean-to shed up against a wall where some geezer used to sell cigarettes and newspapers.

"I go in there and stir up Fatso," he carried on with relish. "I like to spoil his day."

The café was about five minutes' walk from where we were. Steve was in such a hurry I had a job keeping up with him. We got to the café and went inside. As we passed through the entrance, we were met by this seriously large bloke who owned the joint. While I don't want to slag that proprietor off, he certainly needed a lot of room. Calling out to Steve as if he was a friend but what I remember today as the café owner's creepy way of talking to kids - a mixture of patronising parent and sad comedian - there was an uneasiness about the atmosphere between them.

"Hello Stevie boy," slithered the voice of the café owner, otherwise known as Fatso to Steve.

"My name is Steve," my friend emphasised, his voice louder, more resonant, startling his rival. With the grievance of a cobra disturbed in its resting place, Steve reared his head at Fatso, staring him out with eyes that showed only contempt.

"Whatever," Fatso backed down.

The irony of that "Whatever" makes me laugh now. Years later, it is being used by youths to avoid a conversation. If they don't want to listen to what I say they will come out with this.

"Go sit yourself down. The usual fry up?" wittered Fatso in a Spaghetti English accent. From what I can remember I was told, he came from Italy, yet his delivery was more a mixture of Italian, Greek, Spanish, and English.

"What about your friend?" he asked Steve, pointing at me.

"Toast and a cup of tea please," I replied, sitting down quickly. I wanted to get the food out of the way. Steve was still swearing to himself over being called Stevie.

Approximately five minutes passed then Steve's artery clogging plateful turned up with my modest fare. "There you go, Stevie," said Fatso, winding my new friend up even more. Surprised that Steve managed to eat his breakfast without choking, having ranted for half an hour, his restless, unstoppable energy made me want to be free and wild like him. Finishing his meal that he had scooped into his mouth and swallowed with the swiftness of a top competitor in a speed eating competition he gathered himself together announcing: "We're getting out of here before he opens his gob again." Steve wanted to leave without Fatso knowing. He failed. Fatso reappeared, the syrupy whining of his voice raising Steve's hackles. He had been eyeballing us from a part of the shop hidden from our view, waiting to intercept when we tried to escape.

"Going, Stevie? Don't forget we have to pay," he antagonised.

Steve felt inside his pockets for coins. The first shock I had with him was his ability to get hold of large amounts of cash. He pulled his hand out of one pocket clutching a fist full of crunched up paper. I had never seen so much money and it was being held by a fourteen year old kid. Pulling a note from the wad, he threw it on the counter.

"Don't forget the change, Stevie," Fatso reminded. "Stuff it," spat Steve. "Collect what you're owed," I told him. Steve simply said: "His need is greater than mine. Or it will be." This went straight over my head. It seemed a funny thing to say. Later on I realised what he meant. That kind of scene happened there every day but Steve kept going back.

Steve's dislike of being called Stevie was linked to his relationship with his dad. He harboured a strong grudge towards authority figures and acted this out. By calling him that name in the most belittling way Steve's dad had created the conditions for his son's disdain. Steve hated anything to do with his dad. In fact, both his parents rated zero on his scale of importance. If he had heard they were dead he would simply have looked at it as a problem out of the way.

A short distance from the café Steve's mood changed again. He asked me if I would go down the lane with him later. "What's the lane?" I quizzed with naive enthusiasm. "The market, near the Elephant," he answered. "What's the Elephant?" I persisted. "The Elephant and Castle," he explained in a tone suggesting I was stupid for not knowing where we were. Steve expected me to be a walking A-Z. The odd swear word from him followed as a further expression of irritation. "It's a blinking shopping centre. I need to get there before it shuts."

Walking about aimlessly for too long caused our upbeat mood to drop. By deciding for both of us that we were to go shopping, Steve had brought mayhem to our day.

"Come on, that's our bus," he hollered, his eyes following one slowing down to stop. Sprinting in case I missed it left me gasping

- and that was before I smoked twenty cigarettes a day. Steve had shot ahead of me when he first clocked the double-decker and was already waiting by it, restless and irritable. Once on board we were greeted by another extra large person: our West Indian conductor, bigger than Fatso who ran the café - another prime target for Steve's verbal abuse. Scathing with his insults about the conductor's size and body shape, he made heads turn and stay turned. His vile what he called harmless banter challenged the conductor's and everyone belonging to his ethnic group's right to exist. For Steve, not only should they not have been living in this country: they should not have been living. This wasn't a view I shared then and certainly don't now. Then, I didn't know racism existed, let alone understood its twisted logic. Obscene, vitriolic gutter language out of step with his friendliness towards me poured from his lips. Although only words, they were loaded with bitterness. I started to feel tense and slightly paranoid. The impact of the way he delivered them so venomously has stayed with me all these years. There was so much hatred in him no emotional release however big would have got rid of it all. Perhaps ill-treatment early in his life spawned the malice that became part of him. It is not my place to make a diagnosis of Steve's mental condition based on his behaviour then suggest what caused it. I can only describe the effect he had on me.

We sat on the top deck at the front allowing him a decent view of the street below to check if anyone he knew was down there. All the way up the stairs Steve was griping about the ethnic minorities - arguing for their resettlement - and that was putting it mildly. He tossed me some coins and said: "You ask for two threepences to the lane." I honoured his request. Failing to understand Steve's problem with the conductor - the latter laughing amicably all the while he spoke to me, happy-go-lucky - I could tell he loved life. As far as I saw, there wasn't a trace of nastiness in him. Calling me Shorty with an affection I didn't often get outside my family, he gave me the right change. About ten minutes of me putting up with Steve's guided tour commentary on all the shops along the way was replaced by him rising from his seat insisting that this was where we got off. I had no choice but to do the same otherwise I would have lost him. On my reaching the bottom of the stairs and stepping onto the platform, Steve jumped from the vehicle while it was still moving. That made the conductor lose his temper. He shouted at Steve, referring to him as a bloody fool. None of us there could hear what Steve was calling the conductor due to the engine noise and brakes going into crisis as the bus seemingly went from a steady movement to dead stop in the space of seconds. The conductor started talking to me deliriously, too fast for me to understand what he was saying. I don't think he was wishing Steve a nice day. Still not yet initiated into the world of the fast lane, I alighted as soon as I was sure we were stationary.

By the time the bus came to a people scattering halt, Steve was waving at me to get a move on. When I got to him, wheezing, again what he wanted had to be done there and then. He didn't give me leeway to hang on to the little breath I had left. Feeling a pressure on my left arm that was Steve's hand grabbing it with a roughness that surprised me, I found myself being pulled across the road. We started walking down the lane at his frantic pace. He was sporadically looking along the stalls that lined both sides of the street like a small rodent scurrying in and out of the crowd there. The market was packed with activity, vans strewn about, and parked awkwardly, creating minor annoyance to some, notably Steve. I had a job keeping an eye on him. Evidently I hadn't been watching him closely enough. Before I could make my next link, he was shouting at me to run. He yanked my arm with a force that was close to pulling it out of its socket. I noticed he was clutching some clothes and we were being chased by an angry mob. Up to that point I didn't know I could sprint when I needed to. I had this sensation that I was just a body running and my real inner self had been left behind in the market place, still trying to register the contrast between one relatively ordinary experience and another strange and fantastically dangerous one.

From the age of about twelve to thirteen I realised there were easy ways to make money. The seeds of my entrepreneurial skills were beginning to germinate. Starting with a simple milk round that I shared with my younger cousin who had been doing it for a while at one pound and ten shillings Saturdays and Sundays, I progressed to bigger and better things. It was at the lower end of the scale of what I was capable of. Smelling a profitable business in the air, I set about making friends with the milkmen, cutting bargains with them. Deals I organised gave them the chance to have a lie-in. Having enjoyed an extra hour in bed they would arrive ready for work at five a.m. instead of four without having to go to the cold room and load up their floats. Consistently up at the proverbial crack of dawn - without complaining about it - I soon got the reputation for being reliable. It didn't take me long to gain a fair knowledge of all the distribution and collection points, and quotas required. I did most of the vehicles at two and sixpence each for loading the milk, charging a supplementary fee for adding the groceries.

The car washing business came about through the co-operation of a friend in Harlow. Processing vehicles at the market and those of visitors to the shops we could earn fifteen pounds on Saturdays I wasn't able to meet Steve.

Recalling that first visit to "The Elephant" with Steve has stimulated other memories of our later meetings there. It was no coincidence that some borderline to outright criminal activity took place wherever we turned up. On many Saturdays in the nineteen sixties Steve and I had some great times together. During the mornings we would go swimming at the local baths known affectionately to its supporters as the old bathhouse on Camberwell Road, but to the cynics as the verruca farm. It was my view that out of all the visits you made to the old bathhouse you were lucky if you escaped adopting a verruca or suffering a spell of athlete's foot. There was nothing athletic about the way I got mine.

Lunchtime we would stand in line for our pie and mash. Steve found ways of jumping the two queues that used to build up. We never finished our dinner without him quarrelling with someone over something he shouldn't have done. They also sold jellied eels there. Lots of Londoners love them. I wouldn't be surprised if my granddad spent hours at the canal raring for a sighting of his waterborne, snake-like chums. It perturbs me wondering what pain they feel when executed for human consumption. They then have to be boiled so they are fit to eat. That phrase about jellied eels slipping down a treat will never sound the same again. As I see it, the elongated fish are part of keeping the natural balance of the quality and ecology of the river in check. The only thing I can say is that I ate them because Steve did and he was, in today's street cred talk, to quote my granddaughter, Zoë, cool. I had to have lots of pepper and vinegar with mine. You could get them outside pubs in London, usually on a fish stall in a car park. Pie and mash with liquor, on the other hand, was special. That was God's gift to Londoners. The best pie and mash shops were the one at 'The Elephant' and another in Leyton, East London. Swimming in the morning, pie and mash circa 12 o'clock, and the cinema in the afternoon were sheer bliss to us. A few pints of shandy down the line and Steve and some of his cronies who tacked on to him got their kicks out of upending BSA bikes with sidecars.

Throughout my childhood my family and I continued to live at my nan's house in Greenford that was located opposite the iron foundry, a massive place from which I used to watch Indians and people from other ethnic groups swarm when shifts ended. My attitude towards them was one of genuine fascination and admiration.

The women looked nice in their native dress. I saw every one of them as colourful, an array of lovely reds, yellows, and so on, passing by. It was pure brightness and contrasts all at once, and plenty of jewellery, including gold - not that I understood gold then. Gold had real value. I didn't know that as a child. To me it was simply beautiful to look at.

I remember how Steve wouldn't accept I respected ethnicities other than our own. His habit of insulting their cultural distinctness, ranting about the way they formed tight packs in the street or on buses, concerned me.

"Look at them. They're like sardines," was a typical observation of his. To Steve, they weren't his equals. Having no sense of equal rights for white British people other than himself, let alone ethnic minorities, from his point of view they might as well have been another species. He would have been a staunch member of the Hitler youth had he lived in Germany in the nineteen thirties. It came out early on in our friendship that he wanted me to think like him.

I cannot recollect speaking to any black people in Harlow when I was young until this boy joined our class. He stood out for the right reasons. I was intrigued by him because he didn't have to pretend. Of course, in the context of my peer group, he was different yet able to be himself and liked for it. He didn't have to pass in a classroom full of white kids: he was comfortable with his diversity and so it seemed was everyone else. If I had appeared looking and behaving like the girl I convinced myself I was, then in the crude form I called Tammie, I would have stood out for the wrong reasons. Known to my teachers and fellow pupils as a male because that was the sex my body fitted, I would have looked incongruous to my mentors and peers and how they reacted to it would have mattered to me. I wanted to be like that black boy. No-one was against him and no-one saw him as odd or peculiar. They all liked him. I am not saying I think folk should have thought him weird because he was the only black pupil in our form. What I mean is he had a different colour skin and that contrast attracted attention. My upbringing and exposure to Steve's discriminatory behaviour that included his constant bad mouthing of anyone who stood out - spitting, and sticking two fingers up at the world - didn't add up. It led me to believe that had the situation in my class been such that it was full of kids like Steve, that black boy wouldn't have been accepted. If I had shown my true self both in the classroom and at home, I reckoned, from what Steve had told me of his parents' rejection of him, I would have got thrown out.

By this time Steve and I had become good friends. We were close although my connection with him wasn't sexual. Easily led, flicking between naivety and streetwise arrogance, the conceit largely me copying him to look tougher than I was, my teenage self was too busy tasting life's fast lane to notice. He excited me. I fancied him. I had not met anyone like Steve and would bet with confidence that however long I live I never will. I am not sure knowing him helped me. He used to call me "darling". Two youngsters besotted with what we couldn't have and constantly experimenting with new ways of trying to become what we couldn't be, we were almost inseparable. Our relationship was one of infatuation kept topped up with adventure. He was my drug and I was hooked. I needed him. He was my sixties cocaine. With my attraction to him compulsive and growing I had to have my regular fix by going to London nearly every weekend to get it. Potentially dangerous though this was, my ignorance of what he was protected me.

I had known Steve for a few months when my confusion about myself and revelations of his sexuality started to clash with and affect what we had. We were sitting on a wall chatting together, him dominating the conversation as usual. He could be heard from quite a distance. Having flipped about something in his usual manic way, once he had boiled over he paused suddenly. Looking at me with what was for him a rare display of self-control, he said: "You know I'm gay?"

I was young and to me gay meant happy. "I go with blokes," he continued in a matter of fact tone. "At night I visit the city."

Talking to me as if I should have known, he was rattled by my greenness. My first reaction was: "Wow. I know someone who's gay." I hadn't a clue what he was on about. The notion of gay sex wouldn't have crossed my mind at twelve years old. I can't remember being aware of sex in any form at that age.

Physically a boy yet in my head a girl fantasising about adopting the role of Steve's other half without understanding let alone thinking of the idea of us having sex together, my attitude was: "I enjoy your company but I don't want to go beyond what feels safe for me." I had this thing about Steve being my boyfriend.

If only he could have seen me as the girl I felt I was and been a boy who liked girls. To him I was a budding male escort. Even today after all that has happened I am still in awe of Steve, or rather my ideal fantasy of him, that has nothing to do with the real world.

Chapter Four

At about seven years old I began to look for solutions to my unhappiness. When I discovered girls' P.E. knickers there was no turning back. Given the chance, I would walk around in them all day. Soft and green, they felt gorgeous; it was natural for me to want to keep wearing them. I wasn't being spiteful by stealing someone else's undies. They were snugger than the ball-sweltering boys' pants I usually got lumbered with. My fetish continued when I changed schools to an infants' in Harlow. Cross-dressing before I even heard of and understood the term - because it felt right - was only a problem for other people. If I wanted a wee I would use the girls' toilets. There were those rare moments I got stopped by a female teacher or patrolling dinner lady, but that was when I was very young and I could still say I had lost my way and ended up in the little girls' room by mistake. Before the switches threw and puberty let rip - opening the door to the self-consciousness suffered at that stage due to bodies slowly changing into adult ones - it was easy to pass with a lie as obvious as that. The teachers were probably grateful you didn't wet yourself. In any case, the female facilities were cleaner and smelt fresher.

Never standing to go, I always sat on the seat. Mostly it was only possible for me to use the boys'. Now, as an adult, I am disgusted with men's loos. I can trace my dislike of these back to my days of using the ones at school. For me, they are still some of the filthiest places on the planet.

I went to a primary called Waterhouse Moor. They kept shifting my brother Mick and I around. Later, we attended Purford Green in the juniors where we stayed until the summer of 1962. We left there to start at a Secondary Modern that September. At Purford Green if a pair of knickers went missing I was behind it.

During a stretch at the new establishment the usual mix of friends drifted my way. There was one with whom I really identified. I felt closer to her than I did any of the others. Her name was Tammie Martin. When I was with her it was like looking at an expression of my ideal self: how I imagined I would have presented had I been born with the right bits; she came across as strong, assertive, and definitely feminine. There were things I liked about my life then that Tammie didn't have. For instance, I was happy with my family background.

I wanted to be the kind of girl she was yet simultaneously keep everything I liked about my existing way of being that included my will and the values, attitudes, memories, skills and so on she didn't possess which were essentially me.

There is no doubt I was obsessed with Tammie. I used to look at her all day. If I could have stepped out of the male body I was stuck with and into a beautiful female one, to my young mind that would have meant perfection.

This period of my life consisted largely of me doing something I did frequently which was give off the wrong signals, and not always accidentally either for there were phases when I wanted to deceive people. Protective of my alter ego, Tammie, an early experimental form of who I wanted to be, guided by my observations of the real Tammie Martin's looks, dress and behaviour, I flitted between what I saw as my male persona and my emerging female personality.

Remember that I wanted to be like her. The problem was I didn't even know how to look like her. All my efforts bombed. At best, I resembled a second class transvestite. Getting my appearance right had to be done gradually otherwise it would continue to smack of phoniness. I started at a low temperature, simmering away on the back burner for years. As I got older, I turned up the heat until one day I boiled over.

Forced to keep up a gender identity I had been stuck with since birth, that male mask I wore to continue to pass and function adequately in society was only removed on special occasions.

I had to be careful to only let my Tammie self out of her box when it was safe.

Lying became such a habit I did it when it was unnecessary. On arriving home after one of my trips, mum and dad grilled me for the details: I told porkies about where I was and what I did on the day in question, almost all of what I said an invention presented in glorious Technicolor. Having lived the way I wanted in my own wilderness for a few hours without feeling lonely, part of me desired to share that with family and friends. I would claim I had visited the fair and rave about every single ride I hadn't been on. If I had told mum and dad the truth it would have destroyed them. That is why I had to keep shtum about my meetings with Steve.

Being so caught up in those lies I started believing them and acting them out. In my confusion, what Steve told me his mum and dad did to him led me to think my mum and dad would do the same to me.

Steve survived independently of his mum and dad. At that point I couldn't have coped without mine. If Steve told me the truth about this, his parents had thrown him out because he was caught in a compromising position. They had to go and collect him from the police station. When they found out what it was he had been doing they disowned him.

Now I can see how stupid I was. To look a boy, I told my family and friends I had been meeting a girl. I was frustrated to think that for many people I knew I was expected to behave like a male and that was the only way they would approve of me. Recently, mum and a number of acquaintances in Essex I have known for years have told me they would have accepted me as Carol.

My secondary education was a shambles. I didn't learn much. That was my fault. There was little room in my head for mainstream instruction.

Swimming was the only subject I could cope with. I got quite skilled at it. The peace I experienced while I was in the water made me feel whole, like I was in touch with my authentic inner self. I would have stayed in all day if I had been allowed. Every departure from the pool I rejoined the world and carried on with the travesty.

At school I discovered the real differences between boys and girls by hiding in the latters' cloakroom. How I ever got as far as I did without being caught until a few weeks before liberation is beyond me.

Fascinated by the female form, my picture of what it was like to be a girl was sharpening. It was never along the lines of boys peeping at girls through a spy hole. All I wanted to do was study how they looked and behaved in their natural form. When I recall my Tammie Martin persona, I realise how guilty I was of stereotyping. That was my male side trying to be otherwise. I wanted to be genuinely female, not a simulation.

I had my girlie apparel made at a small place down the Old Kent Road. The Jewish tailor who also used to produce Steve's gear was a darling, bless him.

Steve's taste for the good life was gradually rubbing off on me. I found myself wearing his choice of kit. The only problem with this was he could afford these trappings and I couldn't. He did help me address my massive shortfalls, always coming up with money from somewhere. My naive fourteen and a half year old self couldn't have cared less where the dosh supply originated.

I embraced mod culture: all scooters and khaki parkas from the Army and Navy Stores. Rockers were the exhibitionists of leather and motorbikes. I wasn't into any of that. I was passionate about Ford Escorts - the fashion accessory for many of my generation - regrettably too young to drive one legally. I loved mod clothes, basking in two tone mohair that I had in many different colours. Black brogue shoes and Ben Sherman shirts filled my wardrobe and my soul. The tailor used to come out with sayings that cracked me up like:

"Don't worry - it's only a few pounds" which really meant: "many pounds" or "What do you want from me, charity? You can get rags up the road."

For the male role my suits were also mohair. I wouldn't wear anything off the shelf. Willoughby tailors would alter a garment as many times as it needed. My body demanded my togs required several adjustments. According to mum I was so gaunt my ribs showed unhealthily through my skin like some weird percussion instrument you could play similar to a xylophone. Fourteen and a half and wearing a three hundred pound outfit must have been rare. Dreading to think what it would cost today, that taste of prosperity came back to me in a way I can only describe as pride over achieving, if only for a jiffy, adult sophistication in my early teens. It was being smart without putting on a dress. In other words, I really wanted to express myself in a feminine way. This was as far as I could go without being lynched.

Dad had a routine where we stood in front of him to be checked for dirt and lice. It was like a military inspection. The ritual, which took place on bath nights, was dad's method of seeing that we minded the way he had to when he was a boy. Checking every nook and cranny of me and my brothers' bodies for hidden grime - bar our privates - he could be merciless. If you failed the inspection you were sent back to the bathroom to redo what you hadn't done properly, or if he'd had a bad day, the lot. That meant having to have more than one bath - a kid's nightmare. Shoe cleaning had to be executed with military precision. Acceptable wasn't good enough. Shoes had to shine. If they didn't it was back to the tin of polish.

One day two weeks before I left the custody of compulsory education, during the dinner break I sneaked into the girls' changing room. Unbeknown to me I had been spotted going up some stairs by a vigilant teacher. He called the headmaster. A few minutes was enough for me to find what I was looking for - that beautifully laundered uniform hanging invitingly from a clothes hook. Safely outside on the school field wearing her P.E. gear, Tammie, reputedly captain of the school rounders team, was taking part in a practice session.

Handling the uniform with the care of an antiques expert studying a valuable and delicate object, I put it on. The velvet caresses of its material warmed and soothed my skin, bringing it back to life. Unsure whether my quivering was due to my anxiety over the likelihood of being caught or my pleasure from living that moment - which could have been several moments - at least there I knew what being truly alive felt like.

I am seeing this from where I am today; when my young heart was beating under that uniform, the world of Tammie Martin was also that of a child, albeit an adolescent one.

In all probability she would turn out driven and assertive yet throughout her life have those emotional qualities and traits we tend to associate with being female: accepting that some women choose to follow the traditional roles of - in my struggle to find labels that don't offend - housewife and mother, I am implying my view of femininity or womanhood here, and how I would like to be seen that way. I savoured this little sample of Tammie's life she had stepped out of for a short while as if to give me the chance to appreciate it as my own with a touch of the danger I thrived on.

I had just slipped into her attire when I heard voices coming from the swimming pool side of the changing rooms. Treading the fine line between staying hidden and being found, I tried to blend with the clothes hanging on the coat hooks. Another teacher had also reached this sector, cutting me off. Extra support accessed the area via some stairs and I was effectively trapped. That second, my life was caught in freeze frame. I couldn't move but I was able to think. The headmaster shouted at me like a crazed sergeant major. A pair of hands slapped down on my shoulders, shunting me back into the present. I felt sick. That was the fear turning over inside me, making me unsteady on my feet. I was in trouble and I cared. The headmaster's disgust was shown in his strict tone of voice. Harsh comments affected me worse than if I had been punched. I was no longer in control having lost my gift for backchat which I was usually full of whenever I had grief. He was following me closely, his breath touching the back of my neck, the words he said spoken with urgency.

The journey to face justice was uncomfortably drawn-out. I will never forget the details of the corridor and doorway leading to it. The embarrassment of still wearing Tammie's uniform can only be compared to having a football stadium full of heckling youths watching me go to the toilet. Unable to get comfortable, the slightest move I made caused another wave of sickness to roll through me. I wanted to retch.

Arriving outside his office, the headmaster told me to wait. With only ten minutes to the bell when a contingent of students would walk through there to go to afternoon registration, I was worried. I tried to will the minute hand of the clock on the wall near me to go backwards. The inevitability of time moving on and the anticipation of the punishment I was going to receive increased my feeling of powerlessness. Knowing my chances of recovery from this were slim, I was alone in a crowd of hostile kids.

I think some of the roughnecks enjoyed gloating at me, their faces distorted with laughter. Left standing outside the headmaster's office for close to an hour was agony. Tammie and her dad approached me. Her dad's expression looked grotesque, pulled and twisted by a rage he couldn't wait to take out on me. As far as he was concerned I had contaminated his daughter's property. He went to grab me then the headmaster came out. The head greeted Mister

Martin, his uncertain voice barely holding on to its authority. He was angry and painfully embarrassed, desperate to protect the school from further damage. Mister Martin was still shouting at me as he entered the head's office, describing in graphic detail what he was going to do to me when he came out. Through the door, I could hear him ranting at HM. Once the head had used his interpersonal skills to turn Mister Martin's thermostat down the atmosphere settled and the shouting stopped. It was replaced by occasional short outbursts from a slightly raised voice: a gentler but chilling boom that still shook what self-confidence I had. They emerged. Not a word was spoken. Old man Martin and Tammie pushed past me and I was told by the headmaster to get inside.

Almost stumbling in his office, derailed by his strong presence, I flinched when he demanded I stood still and paid attention.

"Don't move," he ordered. I felt like I was dissolving in front of him. He told me I had caused a big problem for both me and the school and that he was considering contacting the police. He kept calling me a thief.

"Look at you," he said, tearing away every last layer of defence I had.

"Who do you think you are?" he went on, shaking with the force of his delivery. "I'm going to cane you, boy."

"Well get on with it," I said to myself.

"Then I'll expel you," he threatened.

I didn't care about being expelled. He warned me I was scheduled to pay for a new uniform. That was daft because, like me, Tammie was leaving in a matter of weeks. It was her dad who pushed to have the one I borrowed replaced. I don't mean he wanted to wear it himself although the thought cracks me up. Old man Martin in schoolgirl guise would be cert 18 for all the wrong reasons. Besides, he hadn't got the figure for it. He wanted me to cough up as a matter of principle. That was his way of getting me to compensate him, not Tammie, for what I had done: I had disturbed the balance of his world. The headmaster wanted to inform my parents. I begged him not to. He struck a bargain with me. If I told them then came back the next day with the money for the substitute outfit, he would see. His offer was my only escape from social death. When I think what could have happened it seemed like I was being let off lightly. On my agreeing to his conditions, he ordered me to report to him the following morning at eight-thirty.

Nothing of this was mentioned to my mum and dad by the headmaster or any school official and certainly not me. I had a fearful respect for my dad. As agreed, I turned up with the cash for the new bib and tucker that could be bought from the school shop. I had to take the money out of my accumulating secret fund. Previously, a small part of the source of that stash was the pickings from what I had believed to be my undetected shoplifting. My mum has since told me she knew what I had been up to. Discovering late in life that I hadn't got away with it shocked me. Her intelligence helped by the fact she was an ally of the shopkeeper, who used to watch and log my crimes, mum proved her resourcefulness. Thanks to their friendship of several years I remained at large. His wasn't the only store where I practised my sleight of hand. I believe I only did his a couple of times, taking a few sweets or small items that mum may have paid for later. I am sure mum would have had a go at me if I had made a habit of it in there. Enjoying a reasonable profit from my weekend car cleaning business I no longer had to bring in cash by using less than honest means. Driven by my desire for money I was always going to get it somehow.

Resummoned to his lair, I found HM cooling off, now more understanding about the mess I had got myself into. His voice was calmer. Happily, it turned out that because I only had a fortnight remaining, and to save Tammie and I anymore woe, nothing further would be said about the incident. He obviously realised that damage limitation was the best option. Rather than let it become an ongoing saga of pain and humiliation he left it as an unfortunate affair to be put behind us. I respect him for that. He told me I could exit the building to find work immediately.

Spending the next two weeks pretending I was going to school hoping my parents didn't find out was like having safely blasted off from a troubled planet then getting stuck in orbit around it.

Chapter Five

When I was in my teens Steve and I had great fun out on the town most weekends. Our friendship had reached a stage where I had accepted he lived for the adrenalin release. If he slagged someone off, instead of showing my disapproval I kept silent.

We made a career out of breaking rules. The stronger I got, the less notice I took of anyone who stood in the way of how I wanted to live. It didn't bother me that at sixteen Steve was already claiming his stake in the world by living dangerously for himself. I followed him around as his willing partner in chaos.

He loved cars. The problem was they were always someone else's. He was into Ford Consuls. The harder they were to borrow, the more he liked them. Occasionally he would keep them for days. Many were left for the police to find. What fascinated him was that the faster he drove them their windscreen wipers became more erratic.

"Look at them. They're doing it again," he would prattle. I couldn't have given a proverbial monkey's how the car was behaving; I was glad to be with him. In the driver's seat he was like a kid with a lollipop. At each petrol station he visited he would tell an attendant to fill up the tank of the car he was using and then ask them to go and get some oil. While the guy was walking back to the station shop, Steve drove off. Probably having nicked petrol from every garage on the A13 in the mid sixties, Steve was a wanted man, though one way of looking at it was that the police would have been pleased when he left the area. Car crime would have plummeted.

Travelling down to Southend in one white Ford Consul and coming back in another that was a different colour - green, black convertible, you name it - fuelled his petrolhead passion for the road. He was always happy if it had gas in it and a Motorola radio installed as he liked to push the great big buttons that were a main feature of this early car entertainment system.

More often than not we would go to Southend, venture to Brighton, or even Hayling Island. Why we kept visiting those places I don't know. I think it was to be with the mods, Steve's preoccupation then. He was a mod of a sort, perhaps one in passing, like me. Now, looking back, Hayling Island was similar to Canvey. Often, I would get a whiff of petrol fumes wafting through the mud smelling breeze; without this it was like Southend when the tide is out and the people are wondering where it has gone and by the look on their faces where they are going. Sometimes it was difficult to get off it as all us visitors seemed to want to leave collectively. Measuring sticks marked off the height of the water in feet. The estuary decided when you left. Take the Isle of Dogs, similar to Canvey. There you had merely a single road near the Blackwall tunnel. As far as Canvey went Steve liked it because the last word of its name was Island. For him it meant seaside and got his marine instinct frothing like the surf of the waves. That urge really amounted to his over excitement about what was a novelty to an urban guerilla like him. Day-tripping to the coast with me was also his idea of being grown up and taking care of me which was lovely of him, especially when he showered me with ninety-nines and candy flosses, plus the odd toffee apple thrown in.

As a child, I enjoyed many happy occasions holidaying at places like Walton-on-the-naze, Frinton, and Clacton-on-Sea; I have a lot of affection for these and other resorts. My dad was the proud owner of a villa that was actually a caravan on a site at Dovercourt.

Nearer home my social life was equally hectic. My friends and I rarely stood still. One day we all went to Streatham ice rink and I had my first taste of real violence. Standing in a group at the edge of the skating arena I was in somebody's sight for a reason that was to prove bad for my health.

He was on the balcony sitting at a table watching us. Hearing a crack, then feeling this pain in my side, I did the best pirouette of my skating career. Once I had finished my party piece, I realised I had been shot with a fairground rifle. In the seconds that followed, bewildered and hurting, I strained my sight in the direction I thought the projectile had come from. Focusing on this space, I saw a boy get up swiftly from his seat and run into the protection of shadows. I recognised him as a lad who had snogged me the previous week. Embarrassingly, I couldn't remember his name. I think it was foreign. He would have been about nineteen. My guess is he wanted to get me because he felt I had deceived him by pretending to be a girl in his company. From the passionate way he grabbed me he must have thought I was a girl and I found it flattering. I never set out to dupe anyone. A nose poker spoiled it by deciding to inform him he had been nuzzling a boy without giving me the chance to tell the truth. What a shame his view of me had to change for the worse because someone couldn't mind their own business.

The events leading up to my first insight into the way I affected some of my fellow Homo sapiens began seven days earlier at the picture house in Camberwell. My friends and I were all messing about in there before we went outside to hang around talking to blokes. That was how I met my assailant and he knew we would be at the stadium the following Saturday morning. Repeating our pattern, after seeing the picture we returned to the fresh air waiting for male talent to come our way.

We had watched this film - I think it was 'the day the earth caught fire' - but as far as that's concerned my memory is a blur. All I know is none of us were interested in it. The cinema was somewhere to go and the movie something to watch. Both were secondary to the fun of being irresponsible in our little teenage girlie gang.

This bloke and I canoodled. So what? I bet that person who ruined my moment just told him matter-of-factly I wasn't a girl. They would have put it like that. Several years down the line and people are still doing this to me. I confided in those I thought were my allies that I was going to have gender realignment surgery, then they took it upon themselves to let everyone else know about it. I ended up being pointed at while shopping in the local supermarket. They told interfering types who were their friends, not mine. The yob who becomes dangerous the moment he gets in a car wants to broadcast the fact that the one thing he can do is drive, the sound from his speakers audio bombing the streets with amplified bass. Passing me breaking the speed limit, the resulting displacement of air almost pushing me over, he wound his window down shouting: "Where's your cock, Carol?" How did he know? Some contact of mine I trusted told him, that's how. Another acquaintance saw me in the supermarket, turned to the person she was with and called out: "There's Carol. She's half and half" and the whispering between them started. Also, the woman on the delicatessen counter at Somerfield calling me "Sir" plus a guy on the frontline at the post office ending whatever he had to say to me with "Mate" informed me they couldn't see me the way I wanted them to. I am never totally free of that question running through my head: do I pass, or don't I?

At the ice rink someone looked at the bit of me that had been hit. There was a hole with a lot of blood coming out. It hurt like a red hot poker being pushed through my skin.

I borrowed a handkerchief and pressed it down firmly on the wound. A taxi got me to the casualty department of the local hospital. The doctor who examined and treated me delighted in saying I had been extremely lucky: the slug had caught the best place for the least amount of damage; for him maybe, but he hadn't got the pain. What he meant was that, for example, if it had penetrated muscle tissue further down, I could have been left with a permanent limp.

Made from a small piece of lead, I stand by what I said that it wasn't a pellet as some of my associates today argue it must have been. Lodged underneath my skin, at first I didn't know it was a bullet. I looked away as the doctor and nurse removed it. Even watching surgeons taking bits out of others in a television medical drama - never mind the fact it is fiction - or, worse still, a documentary, because that is real life, upsets me. You will probably be asking: "How does that square with her saying she's tough?"

I am tough and a wimp then. There's another contradiction for you. Male ego versus girlie vanity. Once I accepted what had happened I became calm. Being shot was all right if you take away the trauma because I got all the glory for bearing that. I wasn't scared when I had some tattoos done. I regretted it later though. Both my arms have these ugly pictures that were scratched on them with sterilised needles. Now I can't wear anything short-sleeved. Colleagues ask me: "What's wrong with tattoos? Lots of women have them." "Yes," I agree, "they don't have these bloody things that scream male at you the moment I roll my sleeves up though." There's a picture of a girl, a dagger, an anchor and other depressing symbols of masculinity.

The young man who shot me was somebody who went crazy because he had snogged a bloke. It got to him; it would most men. I was young and beginning to grow as a person, wanting to be like the girls. They were forming their identities. I needed to. It was all done with their approval. They knew who I was.

I agree that the shooting episode is incredible. Critics will find it hard to understand what followed.

I was driven by the buzz of it. My foe didn't scare me. I had a lot of clothes on and according to the doctor they dampened the impact: I was in a cold place so I dressed for winter. Subsequently, I realised the resulting wound was more blood than injury. One of those big plasters was put on it to protect it. I was still in some pain yet up and walking. It didn't occur to me to go home. A second session at the location of the gunfire brouhaha proved the fact I had been shot raised my status in the group. At the pull of a trigger I had become honorary member. If I hadn't encouraged my comrades to be in the moment life would have revolved around other people's stories. Furthermore, we would have been slagging off our mums, dads, teachers, friends and anyone we considered unusual; there's irony for you. Yet there we were, a tiny community pulling together after one teammate had been struck. There were all these hangers-on in orbit around us fascinated by what we were saying and doing - being, if you like - asking questions. For that moment in that place we were the centre of attention.

We stayed at the rink until about six o'clock. All the other girls I was with met their guys and went round the back for a snog. I found myself temporarily alone in that most romantic of places, the refuse area. Crouched behind a big metal dustbin on wheels close to where

I was standing hid my arch-enemy. He threatened me with a knife. The sound of someone else nearby distracted him. Jumping clear when he lunged the blade at me, I had barely collected myself and he was gone.

Earlier, there had been a problem at the hospital. Staff there wanted to call the police. One of my accomplices said we would get into serious trouble unless we all told the same story. Foreseeing the end of the world if my parents found out I had been attacked, I agreed to co-operate with an arrangement to fabricate the truth. Through talking about it at length we decided on a fictionalised version of events we could all stick to. By telling the hospital staff we did it and that it was an accident we got the strict ward sister's compulsory advice on how to behave. Her bossiness may have been an outlet for a hormonal imbalance, her worst fits of bad temper leaving an emotional wake behind them that made you realise what a woman was capable of if you messed with her. Was this possible example of premenstrual tension in action relieving her frustration by making the sick lay to attention?

Insinuating you only argued with her if you were prepared to risk having a contract taken out on you, she told me I was lucky. That cliché "You're old enough to know better" was foisted on us which we all took great pleasure in ignoring. When she attempted a smile I knew there was hope for her as if her humanity was trying to shine through.

Our spin on the incident was that we purloined a fairground gun and mucked around. It was curiosity and stupidity typical of teenagers.

The injury I sustained wasn't serious. Had it been a high-powered firearm it would have smashed my hip or killed me. In that situation police involvement would have been unavoidable. With the discomfort of the wound hard to put up with, I spent the next few days at home trying to conceal it from my family. Eventually, the affected area healed without further hospital treatment.

As far as I can tell, Steve went after my attacker like a scud missile. When I later asked my friend if he found the guy, he said with a calmness rare for him: "It's been dealt with."

Violence seemed to follow me around. About eight o' clock one summer's evening in 1971 an incident occurred that did involve the police. I had got back from delivering furniture in Wales for a friend who was on holiday. It was a few years before the M25 was built.

Dad came with me to share the driving because we had a large coverage area that had to be completed to a deadline. To use the haulage lingo, we were on a 'multi-drop run'. On our return to Harlow I had to give dad a lift home.

Stopping outside the local pub a short distance from mum and dad's house I felt relaxed having successfully completed the Welsh job. A visit to the hostelry off-licence for a packet of cigarettes led me to walk through the foyer thinking of getting myself a small, relaxing glass of shandy that I never had.

Staggering into my space came this rat-arsed alky stinking of beer, about to lose his balance. Guinness might be good for you, but not the amount he drank. We collided. Trying to keep upright, he swayed back in my direction then quickly regained control of himself to avoid falling over. Frustrated with the slurred sounds he made, the only distinguishable words I could hear were expletives. One moment I was calm, the next full of rage. My anger gave me the energy to push him away, then that sensation of a red hot poker burning into the muscle of the upper part of my left arm warned me I had worse to come. The whole limb felt as if it was alight. Before I freed myself from a cumbersome sweater to find out what he had done he was launching himself at the nearest exit. I removed my top layer and noticed some blood soaking through the material. When I rolled my shirt sleeve up I saw bits hanging out of my arm that should have been in it. Muscle and whatever else holds everything together there was spilling from a three inch slit opened by the knife that abusive lout must have had hidden on him. I passed out.

I remember waking up in an ambulance on its way to Harlow Hospital's accident and emergency department, the person taking care of me telling me I would get fixed.

Medics put back the whole assemblage. It was like they were moving their fingers around in a bowl of spaghetti. Once they had patched me up with the required number of stitches they gave me a bottle of painkillers and advised me to attend a follow up appointment. I was discharged and never returned. Several days later I took the stitches out myself. That is probably why I have a wider scar in that region than there should be. On the night of the attack I was picked up and escorted from hospital by a hunky policeman. His aim of jogging my memory through reintroducing me to the scene of the crime failed to achieve anything other than the sketchy description of my attacker I gave him. We parted company and I drove the lorry home. When I got there the investigation continued. I had to explain my extended absence to my partner Debbie. Understandably, she had been worried about me. I got a grilling that was nothing to do with preparations for the evening meal. When she saw I had been stabbed it took me a while to calm her down.

This and the attacks at Streatham ice rink - which are always linked in my memory - gave me some hard lessons in how brutal human beings can be towards one another.

Chapter Six

In the mid-sixties I started wearing flamboyant clothes to see how far I could go. I believed girls grew up - particularly the extrovert ones - pushing their image boundaries and parents' sanity to the limit. It was their chance to test authority which was one way of finding out who they were, the more outrageous yet still girlie they could be, the better.

Take female rockers in black leathers and boots riding motorcycles. They can be girlie and macho but once they have finished exploring male and female extremes they can tone down their ultramasculine side and settle into being their real selves. Like a butterfly emerging from a chrysalis, out of rough beginnings can come a stable sense of self.

My journey was a bit of trial and a lot of error. Part of that involved the girls deciding what clothes I should wear. I was being trained to their recipe because they wanted me to blend with them. If I had looked weird it would have damaged their street cred. They didn't want to dump me so they tried to make me like them.

I made my own choices based on their advice and they told me if these were acceptable; I let them take the lead. When out with my sisters I was one of the girls, hungry for their guidance to help me on my way. It is because of this start they gave me that I don't have to step in and out of the male and female role anymore. Now I can stay who I am independent of that support.

In those days, if I went off on my own I wasn't quite at ease with myself because my female friends weren't there to rescue me.

On rare occasions I was able to, I adopted the likeness of my alter ego, Tammie Martin, when I was a transvestite of the red-top tabloid kind.

Steve gave me the opportunity to dress in women's clothes as often as I liked, and I did, although I insist that my cross-dressing was never a self-indulgent drag act. It was a necessary part of my becoming a woman. Each cross-dressing session I hoped would be an improvement on the last. Going into a school's female toilet at high risk of being found and punished wasn't done out of perverted lust; it was to be like the girls I admired.

Christine Moon used to say to me: "It's all right for you. You don't have to lug tits around the size of large melons, get the strops, put up with periods every month, and you've got that toughness that gets you places."

There were many statements like that: little half jokes hiding serious concerns. The irony is I am convinced that even then I would have accepted the down side of womanhood these girls were complaining about simply for the privilege of reaching it. At home I had no female mentor to demonstrate and explain all the ins and outs of femininity; it wasn't just about appearance. If I'd had a sister to compare myself with perhaps that would have given me an advantage? My mum was no role model to me because she could only perceive and accept me as a boy. I wanted her to see me as a girl and experience my process of becoming a woman with me. My mum didn't know I was suffering. How could she? I never told her.

My headmaster advised me to go out and be a boy. I turned into a young criminal because I didn't get the back up I required. That doesn't mean I don't accept responsibility for what I did. I rebelled against the lack of empathy. After the way I had been treated, I didn't want anyone's help. From then on I decided I was in control. Whoever got in the way of that would regret it.

Steve allocated me his own brand of consultation. I loved him, or thought I did. Visiting him was like stepping into a parallel universe. There would be that one magic day out of a whole week, the only time I was truly happy. I would go home to my family as if nothing had happened during my weekend trips to London when really it had been total fireworks.

I said to myself: "They're never going to let me be a girl. I'll have to assume a male façade and I'll choose the way I do it." I marked puberty by having these tattoos done. A week later I realised how ugly they looked. I was young and already trying to destroy myself.

You may think I have skipped a bit here. In fact my adolescence ended as abruptly as this suggests. I passed my driving test at seventeen and hit the road getting through a succession of cars. Out of all the vehicles I owned back in the late sixties I had great affection for a yellow Ford Anglia van. It had all the noise of a sports car and the speed of a Reliant Robin. I remember paying sixty pounds for this little marvel with its gear stick that used to start vibrating at about forty miles an hour. It made my hand numb when I got hold of it at this speed or above. The runabout's other irksome feature was the rear doors rattled while it moved.

At nineteen I was a mess. I drank heavily. During one of my calmer periods my first partner came on the scene. I thought: "Why not?"

Troublemakers assumed that because I wasn't married and didn't have a girlfriend I was gay. The unfortunate girl was Debbie. Although I knew I was going to encourage a serious relationship with her, the sensible part of me said I shouldn't because I was doing it to look right. In those days if you were homosexual most people didn't call you gay. You were either a homo or a poof just as if you had learning difficulties you were a moron. I hate those words as much as I do transvestite and transsexual. Even Debbie's mum had discussed my sexuality with her. That was because when Debbie and I were going out together I wasn't interested in the big S. I wouldn't have sex with Debbie; I couldn't have it with Debbie. Her mum was angry that in spite of all those virile young men out there - basically sperm banks on legs gagging to deposit their donations on the spot - her daughter wooed someone who stayed limp for England. Sex didn't work for me. Somewhere along the line I must have managed it because she got pregnant with my eldest child, Tracy.

Tracy was born on the 20th May 1971. Communicating with her about the deeper issues that involve both of us has posed problems because she has found it hard to talk about her past, choosing to avoid raking up how disorientating her voyage of self-discovery has been without a dad. She told me she is not interested in what has gone.

This frustrates me because I would like her to ask me questions: I want the chance to explain my sphere of existence to her. Tracy came looking for her dad and found Carol. That is the way she put it. I appreciate how difficult this was for her. During our heart-to-hearts I am always asking: "Do you want to talk?" All she will say to me is: "I accept you as you are and that's all that matters to us." I keep thinking there is a story here waiting to be told.

Not surprisingly, I was anxious over how she would react to my appearance. Her mother hadn't painted a good picture of me. Tracy mentioned to mum that she wanted to get in touch with her dad and asked her if she knew where he was. My mum answered "Yes" and gave her details of my location but tried to protect her: at first Tracy wasn't informed about my gender dysphoria because she was looking for her dad. In my opinion that was wrong. We discussed it however and decided mum and dad were right. They knew Tracy better than me. I didn't know how to deal with the prospect of a one-to-one, thinking it might be best if I stayed missing. It was then I realised I would want to find out about my biological father if I was in her position. Having agonised over what it might do to her, I resolved to meet her. She had been out of my life for most of hers so she was entitled to an explanation. I asked my mum to tell her what I had done presuming this would help her decide whether she still wished to make our rendezvous, and if she did, soften the blow of what she found. I was told she definitely wanted us to get-together yet I couldn't shake off my concern that on catching the slightest glimpse of me she might want to turn around and back out of the deal. How did I know she wouldn't be horrified at what I had become? That worry was turning over in my mind constantly, along with the thought she might reject me.

If ever I wanted to thank God it was that day in particular. In a way, I wasn't surprised over the similarities between us because when I last saw Tracy I was still with my second partner and remember thinking then how much alike my eldest daughter and I were. Calling to mind our relationship eight years before, at an interval when I tried to reveal to her that I was gender dysphoric and what I had decided to do about it, I smiled over how far we had come. Strangely, I asked her round my house twice during that period. Those arrangements had to be cancelled because I was ill-prepared. By inviting her to meet my second family I risked upsetting the fragile emotional balance there; it never happened. Suffering from a mini breakdown was not the best foundation on which to build a new relationship with her.

In the car on my way down to Harlow all I could think about was what I should wear or, more to the point, what she would be wearing as I didn't want to overdress for her. To look the best I could for my eldest daughter led me to take a suitcase full of clothing and I had only gone for the day. All eventualities hopefully taken care of by the unusually large amount of stuff I packed, I arrived in the morning with plenty of time to fret over the outcome of our encounter.

Tracy got to my mum's at two-thirty. The knock on the door I dreaded came and I might as well have been waiting for a job interview. Instead, I was entering a real moment of discomfort then happiness that would stay with me.

I was sweating so much I was beginning to fear I would need a change of clothes, having one of my hot flushes like the ones described in stories I had read about the female menopause.

Unable to stay in control of my feelings, thoughts, and behaviour, my speech came out all jumbled giving the impression I was suffering from a nervous disorder, with interruptions for several seconds when my mouth moved without any sound coming from it. When the words did return they were still confused, as if I had temporarily gone back to being a child. Most who know me would agree I never stop talking, but then this was my daughter: I was overwhelmed by her.

That first awkward five minutes over and done with, I thought it best we went somewhere private. We disappeared upstairs to a room where we could talk comfortably. For about two hours I poured my life out to Tracy. There were some emotional moments from both of us. At the end of our chat she said a lovely thing. She told me she approved of me. Previously worried that she was going to be faced with a bloke in a frock, who she actually found was a relief to her. Since that day our relationship has moved forward. Tracy has been to stay at my place as I have hers. She accepts me as Carol and what with that and the bonus of knowing my granddaughter - Tracy's daughter, Zoë - a lovely, slim, fair-haired teenager who shares her mother's positive view of my way of being, I am overjoyed. Zoë's first words to me were: "It's cool." That is a compliment in teenagers' language. Zoë has been a guest in my humble domicile too giving me the chance to spoil her.

Tracy has a brother. I can't say much about him because I don't mix in his circle despite the fact I would like to without there being any damage done to either of us.

Missing the world I created for myself in the years before meeting Tracy's mum, I had to retrieve that. I am not blaming Debbie because she didn't know about me. In her eyes I had become a bad person. She couldn't figure out what was wrong. My heavy drinking got heavier. I stayed drunk to survive the day. It was close to my twenty-first birthday when I tried to enlist help. You would have thought that at that age I could have found the courage to put my life in order.

Divulging my predicament in the company of a physician before end stage cirrhosis of the liver kicked in was a wasted effort. He didn't grasp one hint of what I was trying to tell him.

"I fancy men and I like to dress as a woman. What the hell's wrong with me?" I demanded.

It was difficult to say those words. Before I completed my disclosure - impossible in the ten minutes given me - he decided I was homosexual. In his expert medical opinion my cross-dressing meant I was still tied to my mum's apron strings.

He advised me to get a life. That was his answer to my pain. I thought I was going to receive help. All I got was a sense of hopelessness. With hindsight I am being hard on that doctor. I was disappointed and hurt he had summed me up as gay. He hadn't listened to me. It was like nobody understood or ever would understand me.

Chapter Seven

At the end of a busy day, once I got back to the hotel where I was staying I would scrub myself clean. Psychologically, I was getting rid of all that horrible maleness.

Now I don't have to pretend. There is no more hiding for me. During the tricky stretches on the domestic front I found going away to be female an escape from the worst of the pressure. Even so, I was concerned that someone would recognise me as the male I was known as at home and at work. Wherever I found myself I would watch out for anyone I knew.

It was possible for me to stay in as many as four hotels across the country in the space of a week. One of my favourites was near Grantham on the Nottingham road off the A1 that was my main route up north. A husband and wife team ran it. They were a lovely couple. The husband always helped me set up my computer, enabling me to do my invoicing while I was there. I have heard that many gender dysphorics go to a lot of trouble to grab moments being themselves, often pre-dressed for their desired male or female role. I did that to such an extreme that I got close to having a nervous breakdown. The company I grafted for had a garage in nearly every town in the British Isles, which kept me busy.

At many of the stopovers I visited I was able to check-in as male, go to my room, come down as me, and pass as me to management and staff.

I used to size each one up. If I got the right vibe I knew the people running it could take the truth. Occasionally it didn't gel. There were places where I was told: "You're not doing that here."

One day I was in the bar of the lodging in Grantham run by the nice couple. They joined me and together we put the world to rights. It was then I saw my chance to tell them about myself. They had a reservation for a male that was going to be paid for by a female.

The hassle involved with those trips included me having to empty tantamount to the whole contents of my car into various en suites. I had to remove a false floor in the boot which covered the spare wheel compartment to gain access to my feminine clothing.

There was a computer, briefcase, mobile phone, suitcase for dirty working clothes, another for clean and then my special girlie one. I turned the hotel room into an office and boudoir. One side was male, the other female. In that environment - where I was accepted for who I was - it didn't matter.

Once, I nearly got caught out by my workmates who had by chance decided to have a meal at my expense in the same gaff where I was staying. All the bosses of the company my firm worked for and the reps coming down for the merchandising of the garage just completed were present.

Deciding I would have a drink before dinner, I went downstairs to the bar. They were all sitting there laughing; it hit me as if I had copped a mild kick from a low voltage electric fence. Aware of my face blushing with embarrassment, I turned round and left them to it before they recognised me. Spending the rest of the night hiding in my room was the price I paid to save my reputation. Next day they asked me where I was the previous evening. "I was out," I lied. Getting the bill for their indulgence was a shock in itself.

When I first saw Jackie I had to talk to her. Looking at her across a crowded bar supercharged me to act on instinct. She had this charisma that brought her surroundings to life as if they were bathed in bright sunlight. In those first moments of making eye contact with her I could see she was special. I believed this beautiful girl would save me.

Marriage was far from my mind. Savouring every second of her company, I went all out to be what Jackie expected from a boyfriend. She helped me rearrange my life, giving me some semblance of control over it. Through Jackie I had direction and consistency. Drunk during most of the period shortly before I met her, there was little chance I would recover from my alcoholism. It got to the point where I was only working to drink. Immediately after leaving Debbie I moved in with a well-known gypsy family. I knew John, the head of that family, well. John part owned a pub in Harlow. That wasn't the only commercial enterprise he was involved in. I used to help him on his fish stall as well as drive a tipper lorry for his tarmac laying business. That was how I got my money before I met Jackie. I would do anything that needed doing to get drink. I thrived on instability, stepping in and out of my male and female roles, tarmacking macho man by day and, whenever possible, budding girlie by night. Enter Jackie who wanted a boyfriend and girlfriend love each other scenario. This was difficult territory for me. Jackie had to agree that I was useless at relationships. Once we were a couple she decided what took precedence.

"You've got to do this, you've got to do that," I could hear her say without her saying it. "You need a proper job," she advised.

No longer a free spirit, there wasn't much chance of me doing what I wanted when I liked. Every minute had to be accounted for. Marriage means commitment and I accept this; it wasn't long though before I had to ask myself where we drew the line between that value and personal freedom. When were we allowed to follow our own interests without that taking anything away from the love and security of the marriage? Admittedly if she had given me the inch I would have taken the mile. Perhaps she felt she couldn't trust me? My priorities were get up, earn money, and go to the pub. Questions came like knives being thrown at me: Where were you?; Who did you talk to?; Why are you late?; Have you been to the pub?" That was the one she asked me the most. While I was following her regime I smartened up and I accept I have her to thank for that. From being a drunken yob thinking nothing of tarring a road then going to hers to pick her up without having changed, over the course of time she turned my life around. The transformation worried those who knew me including some members of my family due to the fact that much of what they saw me undertaking was out of character. Gradually, Jackie helped me become a responsible adult. Buying the token status symbol car, taking mum and dad-in-law out in it for little trips, were all part of the package. Touring the Isle of Wight with them, carting their Labrador Ginger around, was one of the many features I bought into. I wasn't a dog person. Suddenly I had one. You could tell Ginger was there by his odour. This might have been due to ill-health as he got older.

After him came a golden retriever called Rocky who had a whiff all of his own. Being long-haired it seemed worse than Ginger's. Jackie always had a dog in her life. Following Rocky's demise I bought Sadie for her.

Sadie was an Arabic breed called a Saluki. They are racing dogs bred for speed, similar to greyhounds and whippets in this country.

I lived in a flat two floors up. Sadie worked out how to open the windows and with a kamikaze death wish, jump out. She was friends with the law, used to walking around the inside of Harlow police station as if she was one of the staff. The police semi-adopted her. If I couldn't find her when I got in I knew she was spending the day with the old bill and drove to the police station to collect her. It was like going to pick her up from work. Curious to get to the bottom of her escape attempts, many of which were successful, her hypnotic whizzing around chasing her backside, plus her destructive habits with household furniture, I arranged with her breeder for her to be examined by an animal psychologist - a move that cost money. The diagnosis was that because she had been bred for the outdoors, confinement to a second floor flat in urban Essex had confused her. Perhaps she had bipolar disorder? If she had, according to the animal psychologist's report, the mania bit was set off by us leaving the flat every day for work. Sadie was two bitches in one. When she was with us she was an affectionate, even-tempered animal and, forgive me for going all soft here, from whose lively, soppy eyes shone love. I actually began to warm to the canine world through having her. Unfortunately she had to go. She ate my flat. What do you do with a schizophrenic dog that was one thing with us and something else on her own? Common sense told us that in the end she was better off back with her breeder. One could say Sadie didn't know where she was or who she was without people around her.

In our conversations with each other Jackie had this way of suggesting what I should think. The sentences would be phrased like: "Wouldn't it be a good idea if you took mum...?" which is not a command as such - rather, a strong suggestion with a hidden condition attached to it. If she was annoyed about a request I hadn't honoured I would want to compromise, though sometimes I felt a strong resistance to her opinion. Realising this sense of defiance - that showed itself in my odd moments of irritability - was better kept to myself, gave me a quieter life.

Paying maintenance to Debbie and attention to Jackie were the only ways I could deal with the rapids of my private obstacle course, striking a delicate balance that if only slightly out would find me dashed on the rocks and finished. I objected to awarding Debbie the exorbitant amount laid down by the court. What I was obliged to contribute had only built up through my lack of responsibility. Again Jackie helped me get that in order. Left to me, I would have gone to prison.

Chapter Eight

The first two years of our relationship Jackie and I survived on her money because mine was being used to pay off massive debts I had brought on myself. We weren't living together. Given my financial dependence on her we might as well have been. Johnny the gypsy's place was only a short-term roof over my head. My stay there reached the end of its unnatural course. Dossing down on a shed floor and sitting around a campfire at night was difficult to justify to Jackie or anyone coming from my suburban Essex background. For a short while I shifted back in with my mum and dad. Jackie boarded with hers. Her parents used to feed me periodically. I liked her mum's Sunday lunch. House rules had to be followed. Jackie wouldn't smoke in front of her mum who despised the habit.

It was ages before I could get a pad because I had to clear my arrears with the housing authority. As soon as I moved into my own space I carried on cross-dressing. Jackie only stayed infrequently. She went home practically every night, it being easier for her to lodge at her mum and dad's house, her place of work only a short step up the road from where they lived.

I cross-dressed to feel relaxed. There was no sexual pleasure in it for me and I only did it at those times when I knew I wouldn't be disturbed. It was a closet thing, private to me. I wasn't harming anyone so why shouldn't I have indulged myself? Those cross-dressing sessions were my refuge. Jackie would invariably tell me in advance if she was coming round so I knew there was little risk of her interrupting: I was relatively comfortable to be myself even if it was only in my personal sanctuary.

In due course Jackie moved in with me. I occupied the apartment for about five years. We got married while living there and I still don't understand why. I had already tied the knot once and I didn't like the restrictive lifestyle it brought. Although I kept Jackie waiting for years, she hung on. I know if I was her I would have dumped me within the first month of us meeting; I was no good to her. We could have carried on in the same vein without the ceremony. Most decisions - mainly the important ones - taken out of my hands, the arrangements were made by Jackie and her mum. All I had to do was turn up.

Our first child, Sophie, was born on the 27th July 1983. My Granddaughter, Zoë, has grown up to look a lot like her: tall, slim and blonde. Sophie was a *together* person knowing exactly what she wanted and where she was going. Shortly after she arrived we graduated from the flat to a three-bedroom, semi-detached house we ended up buying.

During her formative years Sophie was a tomboy with her own edge to it no one could imitate. She wanted to hang out with the boys, and she did, beating them at just about anything she enjoyed they happened to engage in. From almost day one she was football mad, costing us a fortune; she used to live in her Arsenal club strip. Maturing quickly, she was a precocious child developing into a strong character, doing well at school, later earning herself promotion at work. By seventeen she held a managerial post with a fast food company.

Ross, second in line, was the young man of the family, obliged to prove himself in an all female household; not an easy task. Sophie talked for him, directing him to do what she thought he should. When our youngest, Alicia, came along, poor Ross was fated to have two assertive little ladies controlling his destiny. With Sophie and Alicia to reckon with trying to mould him into their girlie domain it must have been difficult for Ross to balance that with his need to be a real boy, although his mother and sisters looked after him. I wasn't much cop in that department: I am ashamed to admit it but I couldn't relate to him the way I could the girls. Ross was a lovely, lively boy who tried hard to please everyone.

Later, he became angry. That was my fault. I didn't give him what he needed which was a dad he could identify with. I cannot deny responsibility for the consequences of my absence, leaving when he was eleven. If I had been there during his teenage years I might have smoothed his path to manhood. Ross used to love it when I involved him in what I was doing. It didn't happen often; when it did, the benefit it had on him was palpable. Coming away with me, staying in hotel rooms, he would act grown up and be with me and the men at the garages while we were working. He loved cars and had an exceptional ability to manoeuvre them in tight spaces: Ross's spatial-mechanical skills were remarkable for a boy his age, backed up by the fact he never crashed any, unlike a few of the blokes working for me.

One weekend I took him camping on a friend's farm near our home. I promised him he could use my car on some of the surrounding land which was a large area of cornfield that had been harvested shortly before we arrived. It was a big expanse of stubble. He lived on the buzz from that for months, telling his mates he had spent it driving my motor. The vehicle must have seemed like a big lorry to him. It was actually a large Volvo manual gear change. Going up and down the stubbly terrain like he had always driven - erratically at high speed for this was a roadster capable of well over a hundred miles an hour - Ross churned up enough ground to create his own desert storm. In my imagination I visualised this huge dust cloud advancing in the distance, looking like the trail left behind from several wagon trains shifting across a nineteenth century American desert plain. Ross crammed much excitement into the vacations we had together. There were a few more visits to the smallholding that summer so he could act like a grown up. Suddenly, those rare life packed adventures playing alpha male were snatched away from him. Due to my lack of input, he grew restless. His mother and sisters couldn't do anything with him, each passing day his anger intensifying. At school Ross was often moody and disruptive while at home he behaved rudely and aggressively. That didn't happen if I was around. When I was away he became a different person, hating everyone.

Knowing I have damaged him and that I am no longer in a position to put that right I hope I will be able to say sorry to him one day. That quality of love kids draw from a healthy relationship with both their parents during childhood cannot be experienced the same way when they are adults; then it is too late.

Alicia was always several steps ahead of children her age. Entering the world on the 19th March 1987, she was my youngest and a teenager at six. Committed to avoiding clichés wherever possible, I must employ one here. She was a typical little madam. I used to ask her: "What are you?" and she would reply in her angelic voice, every word well-pronounced, albeit in broad Essex: "A little madam."

Unlike Sophie, Alicia wasn't a tomboy. She loved being a girl, experimenting with clothes and make-up: a young lady who had the largest shoe collection for a youngster. If they had heels she had to have them. With one of the cheekiest faces going Alicia only looked at someone and she got what she wanted. That was a hint of how she might treat her boyfriends when she is older.

I really miss them and would give anything to have them back. All I can do is hope they will contact me.

Chapter Nine

I had these shopping binges. Usually after I had been upset I would spend hundreds of pounds on clothes, then as I was speeding along a country road throw them out of my car window to land in the nearest field. Picture a farmer finding one of his bulls with a designer dress on its back.

I was horrible to Jackie and the children. At one point almost anything Jackie said to me made me angry because she saw right through my defences.

It is hard to explain what went wrong. My partner did virtually everything on the domestic front without complaint: if I got home at one in the morning my dinner would be waiting for me. She put up with me working late most days which showed real trust and an amazing tolerance of my bad time keeping. There would be no coded silences or angry confrontations over my lack of punctuality. Reflecting on the happier moments of my marriage, I realise how blessed I was having a partner who loved me enough to understand me, putting up with the worst of me when the madness took over and I became a monster again.

As she admitted herself, I wasn't the romantic type. I loved Jackie as if she was my sister. She was in love with me. Unfortunately, the me she was in love with bore all the hallmarks of a work of fiction.

I would tell her I loved her, but to me these were simply kind words said by one sister to another: I could never return her affection in the way she wanted.

Latterly, having lost some of my arrogance that had stopped me from seeing a lot of the positive around me, the idea of romance has become more appealing. Still, it is easy to fall for the fluffy image, neatly packaged with an attractive, colourful wrapping that is illusory and my impression of what Jackie wanted our marriage to be. I tried to keep the pretence going by playing the dutiful father, and the obedient husband, interspersed with passing moments of tenderness, while in my imagination I was having an altogether different experience of intimacy with her.

I wouldn't like someone to treat me the way I did her. Today I realise what an advantage it is for me to have the freedom to look back on what I was actioning then, compare that with what I have been through in recent years, and finally appreciate the value of love.

I was being slowly buried alive under a mass of papers with demands printed on them, figures that didn't add up to me, confusing, like the unavoidable conflict between my real inner and social selves. The debts were my obligation. I needed to escape. That made me receptive to Steve's influence. I could have resisted but I wanted to find out where he would take me believing that he might get me closer to the truth about myself. Left to me without the intervention of anyone else, in the end, on the power of my feelings alone, the struggle would have killed me.

At the moment of our reacquaintance I was working in Bury Saint Edmunds doing an installation on a garage forecourt. Bollards had been left at the entrance and exit to stop people driving in and out. Human nature being what it is they still came. There weren't even any petrol pumps on the islands. The arrival of a public that was far from general came with the suddenness and impact of a dam breaking and my past flooded into my present. This powerful voice projecting a flamboyant Cockney/Scottish accent called out: "Tammie," diverting my attention. Right in front of me stood a grinning, red-faced, slender, muscular bloke. He appeared strong. I didn't give a serious thought to him at first. Covered in diesel oil, dazed and embarrassed by hearing someone address me as Tammie, I looked around frantically to discover which if any of my men had heard it. I was about to say: "Can't you see we're shut?" when I recognised him. Steve was back in my life. We last met before I married Debbie.

If my memory serves me correctly, my old friend had attended a beer festival in Bury with his driver, Craig. Like Fatso in the café, seriously big, Craig took up the whole of the driver's side. You couldn't get a cigarette paper between him and Steve: when planning the ergonomics of the driver and front seat passenger area, the designers of the car had not allowed for the possibility of individuals of Craig's build and similar using it, leading me to wonder if they had based its dimensions on a potential customer with the body frame of a whippet in sit up and beg mode.

This charismatic couple reminded me of two gangsters, without the Tommy guns, on their way back to Scotland. We exchanged addresses though I couldn't imagine Steve turning up on my doorstep. I knew if I was in Glasgow I could visit him.

For about six months my old friend didn't really enter my head then I got this job in Glasgow and thought I would catch up with him. A company I worked for had garages all over Scotland, giving me many opportunities to travel there. If anyone in my firm had to go north of the border, I went.

Over the next seven years I made numerous visits to the city. Up there, with Steve, Steve's partner Ewan, and Craig, I found everything I could ask for to be *sort of* me. Unfortunately, it was a *not quite me* me: another virtual reality me, the taint of transvestism still there. Steve knew who I wanted to be from remembering our adventures in the sixties. He accepted I liked to cross-dress and this was discussed during my stays with him and Ewan. I became Steve's idea of me, encouraged to carry on camping when I desperately wanted him to acknowledge that this wasn't his own personal drag act to be performed in front of him whenever he felt like being entertained. I was serious. He knew that but he wanted to put off facing the real issue concerning me. To be fair, we had a decade and a half to catch up with.

One evening when we were sitting together having a drink Steve asked me why I had changed. He couldn't understand that within a few years of losing contact with him I had practically ruined my future by marrying a woman. Defending myself, I told him straight: "You went off and left me."

In my teens he kept my dream alive. I thought he loved me. My compulsion to cross-dress was driven by my elation over being with him. Influenced by portrayals in old films, in my virtual reality world I was a gangster's moll, finding great comfort in this. Steve was moulding me into his own fantasy figure. While that was happening Steve and Ewan's relationship, whatever it had been, was breaking down. The atmosphere between them changed from the moment I was in Steve's life again. If I was there Steve would ignore Ewan unless he was telling him to do something. Ewan would speak and Steve would carry on talking to me as if Ewan wasn't there. That made me uncomfortable. I was coming between them. It was all me and no Ewan. Ewan was given his orders then commanded to go. I didn't want it to be that way.

Although I could have stopped it and I should have, I didn't. Ewan was reasonable. I felt sorry for him. Steve gave me material things I said I liked: clothes; jewellery; money; and so on.

During 1988, on the strength of several visits from me, Steve and Ewan decided they would convert a room on the second floor of their house for my use. Given a selection of three I chose the middle one which used to be territory best described as a large upstairs lounge. Four weeks later I re-explored this, transformed into luxury during my absence. The bare coldness of non-use with drab brown wallpaper and maroon walls I worried were giving off toxic fumes through the lead in the paint, and heavy old curtains that just by me looking at them made me feel even lower than I was in my darkest moments, had gone.

My quarters, about thirty by twenty feet in overall size, had an en suite bathroom on the left as I walked in. A modern gas burner for a coal fireplace fitted the old style hearth without taking anything away from its period charm, evoking a chimerical image or two. Staring at this wonderful structure, then, for a short while, looking out of a window down on to the wide, roomy street below that was the Hamilton Road which extended into Glasgow city centre, I conjured up a dreamscape of horse drawn carriages rattling past with the gentle clip clop tempo of those lovely animals' hooves, quietening the nerves and steadying the hearts of those privileged to hear such a familiar, reassuring sound.

These days, at its worst, the street had heavy traffic clogging it: an example of early twenty-first century chaos upsetting the balance of a once relatively peaceful area. In my room, with that fireplace the old went hand in hand with the new. Arguably, that was the one location in the whole house where the genuineness and honesty of the antiquated - practical, yet at the same time attractive - was comfortable around the contemporary. Without all the mess and work involved in lighting and keeping the traditional coal fires burning, the modern came into its own. The instant, ready-made glow, followed swiftly by the hypnotic motion of the flames flickering, slow-dancing above the coals, seduced me, drawing me deeper into my world of becoming.

Recalling my classy pad in its entirety, almost the whole length of one wall was made-up of built-in furniture. Halfway along it there was provision for a bed and then the wardrobes carried on. At the far end, although it looked like part of a cupboard, I used to open the door to find a walk-in office complete with its own telephone. Apart from the historical touches, the house was innovative. Thick carpets, lowered ceilings, recessed lighting, pictures or tiles illuminated with a soft glow added to the dynamic. It was a plush executive room that cost a lot of money. The bed was like being in the cockpit of an aircraft. You could do all the lights and everything lying down if you didn't want to get up. I know it sounds a bit seventies from an episode of Jason King or one of the James Bond films. Steve, Ewan and the contractors were being creative. With enthusiasm and energy they took on and played out this role, turning that space into my living quarters. I felt valued and safe.

From 1987 until circa 1994 my association with Steve was friendship and fun. He encouraged me to take part in his macho activities. Despite being gay he had episodes when he appeared to be a girl loving macho male of the tarmac. We shared a passion for motor racing. I hadn't lost my desire to be out there getting high on the slipstream action of the racing circuit. You could smell the fuel. I thought I could spot Steve sniffing hungrily at the air, drawing its aroma through his nostrils to get high. The horrendous power of the super bikes I rode on those speedway afternoons Steve and I enjoyed was a jet-fuelled heaven, recreating the buzz I got from pushing a formula one car to its limits around a race track.

Now in his forties, Steve's outlook hadn't mellowed, being, if anything, more extreme than that of the fourteen-year-old boy he was when I first met him. To him some of the locals were what he called jockstraps who made fair skivvies for a bit of beer money. Probably believing he was Scotland's answer to the Krays, he and Glaswegians were a lethal combination, like putting two highly combustible materials together.

His anger and paranoia were disturbing. He had also developed his own version of a Glaswegian accent that reminded me of the television character Rab C. Nesbitt.

Steve and some of his hangers-on - or mates - I don't know whether they were his real friends - had their own subculture. They believed that under his guidance - as long as they stayed loyal to him - they were safe from other people who were the same as them. In a way, they were part of his health and safety insurance policy. Although they benefited from their connection with him the advantage was largely his. He always had money, which was what attracted them to him; he became their bank account and controlled what they had. Buying friendship was second nature: if he liked certain characters he would give but want a return on his investment; if he didn't he would let them know. There was no question of me or anyone being able to defend the unfortunate person he wanted to sort. With a strong, robust body, plus stamina and allure to match, his form challenged the gay male stereotype. He didn't do weight training and probably had no idea what it was. His strength was greater than his physical appearance suggested, primed and driven by years of resentment concentrated inside that small but powerful frame.

My mum told me I had too much aggression in me. It wasn't mine. I was acting out stuff that was really Steve's, picking it up off him, becoming one of the many channels for his anger. Like getting a bug and suffering its symptoms, bits of Steve's negative energy broke off his aura, found mine, and clung to it. Sadistic and uncompromising or kind and generous, Steve's presence could be felt by those he had close business or personal relationships with.

His hangers-on had to test the ground before approaching him. They could never be themselves with him in the room. In his eyes, they existed as mere extensions of himself. If someone upset him Queensberry rules didn't apply.

Gradually, I noticed changes in Steve that worried me. Like any physical expression of love, to me gay sex was the business of consenting adults who fancied each other. Perhaps I was naive, I don't know? Up to approximately 1994 I never thought Steve would openly disregard my boundaries. He was part of my history. I was troubled that this didn't stop him trying to get off with me. It was hard to accept that a pal I trusted who was gay wanted me to sleep with him when he knew I wasn't interested in him that way.

"No matter what you do you'll always be a bloke," he insisted.

He wanted me to be the gay male transvestite I was in his fantasy.

Chapter Ten

Weeks had passed since my reunion with Steve at Bury Saint Edmunds and I still hadn't found the courage to tell Jackie who I was. Instead, I built this wall of hate between us to distract her from finding out the truth about me. One day I concluded it was easier for me to quit. Thinking that if I could make Jackie resent me my leaving would be less painful for her, I said some hurtful things. I am afraid it looks like a pathetic plea for forgiveness, but I didn't mean them.

Visiting Russell Reid for a consultation at The London Institute, Warwick Road, near Earl's Court, to help sort my head out gave me such hope until I discovered it was all private. A general practitioner found Doctor Reid's name and practice address. He recommended I went to see him. An appointment was made and I ended up in front of Russell kitted out girlie style: bangles, dangly earrings, painted fingernails - things I now detest. Russell was a nice man: polite, sympathetic, his professional manner that of a gentleman. I looked upon him as a friend rather than a psychiatrist.

"Hello Carol. How are you? Come into my office. Now tell me what's happening," was his welcome. For once I knew I wouldn't have to put up my usual defences to stop myself from being hurt. I didn't consult him again until about 1997.

Technically, I was not actually resident at the family home for one period, although I was there probably more than I had been in the previous few years put together, going back regularly to check if Jackie and the children were all right. Still working, paying the mortgage on the house, with hindsight both that plus the fact I was missing them made my moving out a pointless exercise, except for giving me a tough lesson in how important they were to me.

Jackie thought I was staying with someone else. Actually, I had taken a six month lease out on a flat near Southend.

I had lived at Leigh-on-Sea a few weeks when I faced an eventful day. Early one morning, turning out of my street on to the main road, I stopped at a set of traffic lights which stayed red for a long time. I noticed a police car pull up behind me. My then current set of wheels had only been serviced the day before, so if, as I thought, the police were going to apprehend me, it shouldn't have been because it was showing structural or functional problems.

Green displayed and I carried on. I had got across the A13 when I saw a spectacle of blue flashing behind me. A siren urged me to pull over. Expecting trouble, I pushed the button for the window on my driver's side to go down. A policeman peered through the gap. He politely asked me the predictable question: "Is this your car, Madam?"

Without hesitation, I replied: "Yes, officer."

Given I was dressed as a female with the voice of a scrum half no wonder he looked at me gobsmacked. He must have stood there for about thirty seconds before he said anything else. When his brain switched back on he asked me if I had any documents. A shock equivalent to being struck by lightning, followed by panic, turned me hot and flustered; at least I am pretty sure that wasn't down to hormones. Nil desperandum. I had my certificate from Russell's clinic that said I could dress in a way that fitted my desired gender role. The interrogating officer kept looking at me, then my driving licence, closely followed by the testimonial from the clinic. His face mimed the phrase: "This does not fit the norm." He returned to his wagon to discuss the "I don't know what to do bit" with his colleague. I knew that with the intention of cross-examining me they would have radioed their base for a vehicle check while sitting behind me at the lights, and subsequently informed that the car was registered under a male name. These jobsworths ruled they could arrest me for impersonating a female. At first I wondered if my Volvo had seduced them. It was a twenty-four valve fuel injected job. Massive, resembling an aeroplane without wings, to me, as it accelerated, it almost took off like one.

What might have started as my pursuers' curiosity over my car ended up with me being seized. If anyone knows Leigh-on-Sea you don't leave a thirty-five thousand pound luxury motor in one place for too long because somebody will decide to remove it for you or damage it trying. No matter how much I protested, the potential auditionees for 'The Bill' decided I must go with them to Southend police station. The guy who came to my car first kept calling me by my male name which was on my driving licence, although the document from the clinic clearly stated that the one I used was Miss Carol Royce. Once we had arrived outside the station I got out of the police vehicle and the same officer said: "Mind your wig, dear."

Having been taken to this dull room and told to wait, I wasn't happy. Gone for about thirty minutes, the police escorts seemed to be making me hang about, then when one returned to tell me I would be there for a further half an hour and asked me if I wanted a drink, I felt relieved. "What's the problem?" I asked. "We're verifying something," was his reply. It was about an hour before I saw the coppers again. Being made to wait to be charged with whatever they could lay on me made me angry. They had no reason to treat me like that for legally I had done nothing wrong. I suppose I ought to show gratitude I was put in an interview room and not a cell. Unhappy over having spent two hours of my life sitting in a police station for the cause of British justice, I felt the least those officers could have done was explain to me why.

Chapter Eleven

Thanks to a friend of Steve's, in 1993 I visited the Albany clinic in Prestwich, Manchester, arriving there in an anxious state. The Albany is a fully-equipped private medical centre that provides advice, support, and treatment for transsexuals. Everything needed for a successful transformation is under one roof.

I remember turning up in my car on the first morning looking for a small hospital, finding the address I had been given and being faced with a big metal grille that looked like an object out of the Falls Road in Belfast. All that was missing was the razor wire and the searchlights.

If you arrive as early as I did on my introductory visit don't be put off by this. The kindness and support you find inside will make up for the grimness outside.

As soon as I entered the building I felt secure. The female staff treated me with respect. That made it easy for me to talk to them. Apologising for coming through the door as a male helped me establish a positive relationship with them from the start: humility, politeness and openness are qualities I value highly that build bridges of communication and co-operation between helper and helpee.

I realise how money gave me the choice to go there and no doubt had an influence on the way I was treated; I still felt the girls cared about me. What made the place work was that it was run exclusively by women. There was no need for me to prove to them I was female. They accepted this without question. Jill used to listen to me go on for hours. She had this way of making me feel better. Back then I was a sad case full of self-pity.

The other person who helped me was Marion. If Jill wasn't available I inflicted my angst on her. Both these girls saved my life. They were the first women I spoke to about my gender dysphoria who listened. I owe them a lot; I suppose I relied on their goodwill.

My operation had been booked for around 1995 and then my money ran out, slamming the door shut on this option. I could not afford to be treated at the Albany anymore. Grateful to the staff there for what they had done for me up to that point, I accepted this without resentment. It was a business. I was running my own in Essex; I appreciated that like me they had to make money to survive.

I began to read what I could about gender dysphoria. Jill and Marion encouraged me, knowing where to look for books which didn't call for a dictionary to understand them. I have since learned I could have received hormone therapy in my teens, delaying puberty to avoid the pain of becoming a man by staying a boy until I had my operation. One might say I could have been eased into womanhood rather than booted into manhood. Joining GEMS[1] to get to know other gender dysphoric people was a big step.

A lot of the social stigma attached to gender dysphoria comes from fear through continuing ignorance of the facts. Until that is reversed, those designated male at birth subject to the condition are in danger of being unjustly dismissed as both the perverted and the perverting. Items I read sent me ballistic such as the claim they are not really female because they require hormones and surgery to be so. Of course, the critics don't have the affliction. It has been said that when their youth starts to fade and the masculine role no longer works for them male gender dysphorics want to change sex. They can then use the female role to increase their opportunities for a better life as women from middle-age onwards. This attitude rubbishes the necessity of many to achieve their true identities and the argument that gender realignment is not a simple matter of lifestyle choice. My world had not ended because I had reached the menopause. Playing male would never be the best years of my life.

The path I chose brought in good money. I could have minced around an office all day but would not have earned much. My job was a profession that even in the 1970s and 80s posed cultural difficulties for biological females who wanted to follow and sustain it. Yes, the male role did allow me to enjoy a decent standard of living for many years. As I keep stressing though, I have always been female, with some useful masculine traits to my advantage.

Thankfully, the arguments put forward to justify disallowing the alteration of post-operative transgender people's birth certificates were being seriously challenged in the early noughties. *Newsnight* carried an item concerning this broadcast on Thursday 11th July 2002. A reason for not being allowed to alter my birth certificate to reflect my newly realigned gender was: "If you suffer or in the past have suffered from gender dysphoria everyone has a right to know about it." Following realignment, former gender dysphorics like me are only trying to lead a relatively settled life that cannot be achieved if our previous history is still visible to certain others.

Appearing on a television programme convinced me that its makers had invited folks with gender identity problems to a media bear pit deliberately stirring up negative public reaction; the edition I attended was the equivalent of throwing petrol on a fire. They were warming up for a riot in that studio, the producers loving it. The deluding and the deluded went on stage to be slagged off by those in the audience who were largely a bunch of hypocrites. Men dressed as women allowed the make-up department to go overboard. If you are a man, put a dress on, go to the pub, then act male, you could be laughed right out of the place. If you want to pass as a woman you have to behave like one. When a guy enters a room and catches a glimpse of what seems to be a girl in both physical appearance and dress, for a nanosecond he will almost certainly accept what he sees because on the surface it fits the information he has stored in his brain as to what are the most basic features a person must have to look female. For a few ticks the male observer probably decides this is the case: after his initial impression, received in a flash, watching how they talk and behave for a longer period adds to it, either weakening or strengthening his idea.

When my co-writer David Berthelot met me in 1998 he knew nothing about gender dysphoria or transsexualism as it is better known. Like me, he found portrayals of male transvestism absurdly camp: pantomimic exaggeration parodying and almost defeating the object of the exercise. While I could appreciate how the look and behaviour of a minority would attract critical comments, others may be enduring pangs of guilt over enjoying cross-dressing. They are usually men who feel the urge to act out their idea of being a woman by dressing up in women's clothes that may result in them getting sexually aroused and climaxing.

David had heard of the word transsexual and assumed that people labelled this and transvestites were virtually one and the same. Transvestites are apparently fetishists. As we shall reveal though, it is not that simple. It is true that, in general terms, transvestites do not want to physically change sex; however, the dividing line between transvestism and transsexualism may be blurred. Can transvestites become gender dysphoric? Obviously some don't want to change. I myself believe that in several cases the wife or partner knows. There are transvestites who start their cross-dressing career wearing female clothes that are desperately over the top: wigs you can't miss and gear in colours that literally scream tranny at you. Once they have gone to those extremes to push the boundaries of what is socially acceptable as far back as they can they may become comfortable with their female personas. Their cross-dressing settles into a manner based on reality; they tone it down so their appearance is more subtle, which may be accepted as naturally feminine. Transvestism is tolerated by specific employers who will allow an employee to practise it as part of their working life: males who dress modestly as females in the workplace can be brilliant at their jobs because they are able to successfully blend their cross-dressing with their professional role. These individuals are happy to stay physically male but want to express the strong feminine side of their identities by regularly adopting a female persona because this way they feel at their greatest ease.

There are those who after spending years being a transvestite discover it is no longer enough for them. It is then that they seek gender realignment. They had probably always been gender dysphoric, perhaps at the beginning too frightened to confront it, turning to transvestism instead as a halfway house until the emotional disturbances inhibiting their desire for a proper resolution settled.

One shrink told me I was a transvestite. When I objected to this he said I should know what I am. The fact I didn't follow the national health route right from the start made me one as far as he was concerned. If you don't want to be labelled 'transvestite' you must follow textbook procedure by shutting down your old life completely without going through the preliminary stages developing your self-awareness naturally, a process that differs in character from person to person. The NHS way is only a fraction about this and mostly about following rules. On the one hand, I knew who I was, on the other, medical professionals were telling me what I had to do to be who I was.

In the eyes of this psychiatrist, I wavered between dressing as a female in places away from the family home and work, and being the good male I should. To him, then, I was a transvestite: a man in drag.

What the television programme I was on did show was how gender dysphorics tend to be judged with little or no attempt made to understand their frame of reference.

Then came the phrase that summed up the stupidity of most of those populating that studio, the words of a smug individual who had been rehearsing them in his head until at last he found the moment he could claim his thirty seconds of fame by delivering them at considerable volume. "Babies need operations before transsexuals have their willies cut off." Sorry, he meant to say male-to-female transsexuals. Females-to-males want one, don't they?

The producers were not interested in using the airtime to discuss how complex and tragic gender dysphoria is. They could have encouraged a balanced debate on it. If audience members felt that disgusted with the issue, or found us funny, then I am more than worried about our society.

This narrow-mindedness can have serious consequences. At the moment of writing, I believed that a constructed, or as I preferred to call myself, realigned female, was inadequately protected by the law. A realigned female was not considered authentic. If she still exhibited some male characteristics such as a deeper voice than expected, was assaulted, and reported the attack to the police, she was vulnerable to the criticism that she attracted the violence because she appeared and sounded like a transvestite and therefore probably asked for it.

My femininity was real enough to me. With the medication from the Albany my body took on a more female shape. I began to develop breasts. My face had a softer outline. I noticed my hair - once bombardment by the evil testosterone slowed down - looked smoother and silkier. My body movements, that had to be learned and refined, became noticeably feminine. This part of the transformation is probably the hardest for gender dysphorics. In my youth, a lot of households saw mum teaching her daughters how to act female and dad instructing his sons on the rigours of becoming a man. I wanted to unlearn the male role I had been socialised into. Experience showed me that unless I suffered total amnesia there was no way I could achieve this. Although I had many male traits Jackie often picked me up on the way I did things because I didn't do them like a man.

"Why are you standing like that? Don't wear shorts," she would demand, because I had girlie legs and she thought the weirdness of these would have a bad effect on her image. I don't know whether I copied it from other females without realising it, that it came naturally to me, or it was a bit of both, if that makes sense, but when I felt relaxed I stood like a woman. I didn't have to think about sitting or standing like a woman then. It just happened. That is what I meant when I was talking about the left and the right hand. People saw me do everything right-handed. That right-handedness felt unnatural: I wanted to be left-handed, which was the correct way for me. I had to suppress that for the sake of looking right, especially for Jackie because if I didn't there would be a row. Sometimes I might forget and behave my way then she would criticise me for it, leading me to go on the defensive causing us to clash.

While honing the finer details of being female I battled with the medics who were treating me. I gathered they largely saw me as sick even though I was able to make rational decisions and run my own life.

I had to be referred by my doctor to a psychiatrist at Charing Cross Hospital, a second psychiatrist and a gender counsellor in Norwich. If I could not convince these who I was then I didn't stand a chance.

Certain doctors appear to fall by accident into the wake that gender dysphoria leaves behind it to become involved in more than the medical side of its process. One of mine said that while he found the condition interesting he knew little about it.

When I visited Charing Cross I only saw male psychiatrists whose idea of femininity tended to be outrageously stereotypical, unless they were checking my reactions as part of the real life test. One made a remark about my appearance.

"I see you're wearing trousers. That's not very feminine, is it?" he sneered.

"Women wear trousers a lot these days. We're about to enter the twenty-first century remember," I retaliated.

"My wife doesn't. She wears nice skirts. I think that's very feminine."

That got my hackles up. Following a bit of verbal sparring with him, he told me I was argumentative and that real women didn't argue with their men. I think the fact I was twenty minutes late for the appointment riled him. When he challenged me over my lateness the thought flashed through my head that it was a woman's prerogative to change her mind or be late.

He would have probably come back with the remark: "Come on, you've got a penis. You must be male."

It is unlikely these therapists will ever be able to empathise with those who are gender dysphoric. A friend in Romford had been waiting ten years for realignment. She went backwards and forwards to Charing Cross. Unable to convince her psychiatrists she was genuine because she couldn't satisfy all the criteria laid down in some manual, being unemployed, living on income support and generally isolated, there was nowhere for her to go.

Note

1 GEMS is 'The Gender Society', provided by 'The Gender Trust', which is a helpful organisation for gender dysphorics who want information, a contact network, befriending, or referral to a trained counsellor.

Chapter Twelve

Steve had connections with the pop music, fashion, and sporting worlds, pushing his way into the lives of those he thought would be of use to him. I called him the groupie with attitude. Clearly, he influenced the people he idolised and got them to do what he wanted. He ran the master class on how to mix business with pleasure.

During the summer of 1994 it was decided that Steve and I along with his back up mob would fly down to Margate. Steve reshuffled his minions regularly. Manic conversation and laughter abounded. We became the crazy team in his aircraft which we called the gang bus and was kept at Prestwick airport. He liked to tell everyone he knew that he was in possession of a plane, even if it was only a bit of one. I think he owned a few of the rivets holding it together. It was his status symbol. His friends had fast cars, he had his aeroplane.

On the day, we got to the airport at about ten. It was a warm, sunny morning. When we reached the gang bus, the engines were purring as if they were in ecstasy over Steve's sexy pilot, Doug, doing the preflight check on them. This was the foreplay before the climax. You might say that from a distance I was doing my preflight check on him while he was talking to the control tower on the aircraft radio link.

Steve was ranting at Doug: "Why have you got the engines running? That's costing me." Doug would whisper to himself, smooth as Irish coffee: "Get a life."

Doug was the cream of the Irish race, a thoroughbred, his black hair combed back as smooth and as glossy as the coat of a cat that had been well looked after, showing up nicely when the sunlight of that glorious forenoon shone on it. His vagabond face, his deep blue eyes, his charm, made him the perfect young Irishman. He had mannerisms that made his Irishness sexy. His personality - and he certainly had one – was present and real compared to the others who were there, including Steve. He was like a sentence on the page of a book that stood out and hit you; he had a special way about him. I admired Doug, Jackie, and Steve because they all had charisma. Doug's was exceptional though. My recollection of him still fills me with this fantastic warmth. In fact, thinking about him gives me goose bumps.

I don't want to leave this memory; forgive me if I draw it out, savouring every detail like when I am watching the dishy barman of an Irish pub in Essex slowly pull me half a pint of Guinness on a scorching hot day.

Doug stood about six feet tall, was well proportioned and mega muscular, with similarities to a body builder. I am still besotted with this Adonis of Irish masculinity. Talk about bend me, shape me any way he wanted me. I meant that as an invitation from me to him. I would say he was probably in his early thirties then. Before coming to England he lived in Belfast.

Once we were airborne Steve was on the turn, sitting in the co-pilot's seat pretending to supervise the flight in dictatorial mode yelling: "Shift it Paddy. I want to get there today."

I think the plane was procured by one of these syndicates that about twenty people had shares in. It was a nice one - not that I know much about this type of transport - accommodating up to ten or twelve passengers: a twin propeller job, posh inside, with leather seats. It had a well stocked bar which I thought was dodgy. Booze and aircraft could be a lethal combination. Knowing Steve and the drunkards he used to hang out with, if we were going to crash he would say: "I'll grab the malt" before bailing out attached to the only parachute on board. Doug said his aerial miracle would glide if necessary unless it was blown up or vital bits of it fell off during the flight. It had two engines but could be flown and brought down safely on one.

"Don't worry, Carol. I counted the bits before we took off and they were all there and looked stuck on properly," was an example of Doug's wit. He was Mister reassuring with a sense of humour. According to him it was safer than a helicopter. Until Doug told me this I was under the impression that if the engines were cut it just fell out of the sky.

"Carol," I thought to myself, "If you're going to die at least you'll have someone sexy with you when it happens."

We had only been in the air a short time when I asked Steve if I could sit at the controls with Doug. This was like telling a small child I wanted to play with his favourite toy. He went into one before giving up his seat saying: "A quick go."

"He'll suck his thumb in a minute," Doug commented. We both laughed together, excluding the others from our thoughts as if we were sharing a joke that only we understood. That made Steve jealous and he let us know it. He was hilarious. "Speak English you Irish git," he said.

Doug had this lovely broad Belfast accent. His words blended beautifully, flowing in an almost musical way. Making me crack up with the things he came out with - his 'little ditties' as he called them - he would start by saying: "Back home…" suggesting he was about to pick up and strum an acoustic guitar then break into song telling some gem of Irish folklore to a fascinated audience.

About an hour into the flight Doug switched to autopilot. He vacated his post telling me he was going to the toilet that was in a room the size of a broom cupboard. You had to really want to go to risk using it.

"I won't be a minute," he muttered quickly, the speed of his voice revealing how desperate he was. "Be a good girl. Don't touch anything. She'll fly herself," all this said in one breath. For me it was like sitting in the front passenger seat of a car doing over a hundred with no driver. A funny feeling somewhere between joy and anxiety caught me off guard when I looked at the mass of gauges stretching across the width of the cockpit, glowing with an eerie, luminous green, expecting them to start flickering like mad then fall to zero. Leaving gadgets in charge of lives is not a great idea. My car had cruise control. I still had to steer it. How, I don't know, but at some point I must have touched or kicked a serious bit that flew this fancy crate because suddenly the receiver erupted with swearing. For once Doug beat Steve when it came to delivering obscenities.

He came charging back into the pilot's cabin, adjusting his trousers frantically, almost catching his pride and joy in the zip. Removing all the f words from his outburst, if my translation of what I remember him saying is correct, I think he meant: "What have you touched?"

He was not a happy man. I avoided any quips about my cock up in the cockpit and his untidy appearance through being interrupted midstream. Settling, he started correcting the imbalance I had caused, giving me a lecture filled with expletives on how I could have killed us all. Delivered partly in Irish, it was more funny than upsetting helped by the fact he didn't stay angry for long. I knew he was mellowing on recounting to me that he had felt some irregular turbulence when otherwise engaged and worried I would lose him his licence. Taking the aircraft off autopilot was remarkable given my lack of aviation knowledge. Probably my temptation to fiddle with controls, believing that whatever I touched would remain steady, helped it on its way. All that and I was only looking for Radio One.

Doug asked me to sit down in the passenger area as we would be landing shortly. To avoid bringing him back to the boil I got up and reinstalled myself where I had been at the beginning of the jaunt. Following touchdown at RAF Manston during taxiing to our allotted parking space, Doug told us in his lilting Irish tones that our departure would be eight p.m.

Transferring to a people carrier like a group of small children moving in single file, getting on in disbelief at the trouble Steve had gone to, makes me laugh now when I look back. I mean, why? I have often wondered if it was all a theatrical exercise, written, produced and directed by Steve, in which he played the lead to prove to himself he was number one, the vehicle, a posh Japanese minibus, another prop he demanded to buttress his ego. There would only be one performance of this show and the many others that followed.

Leaving Doug behind at the aerodrome to secure and watch over our aerial conveyance - a definite anticlimax - Steve ordered our driver to proceed.

In Hythe, we pulled up outside a pub. Our guts groaned and gurgled the basic notes of what could have become the world's first gastric symphony. To say we hoped they did food other than a piddling bar snack cobbled together from the day before's left-overs is an understatement. Steve was brokering a deal there. All of us full of nervous energy through being hyperactive from the flight, we found it difficult to keep still. I was starving and couldn't have cared less what Steve was doing. A couple of the lads and I made for the restaurant to order some of the expensive items on its menu.

As Steve was paying we racked up quite a bill. Making the most of this opportunity by ordering steak with the trimmings plus drinks, encouraging my acquaintances to do the same, you could say we went out of our way to enjoy ourselves. At the end of the meal we were blobbed. Steve and Craig didn't eat with us. They were busy haggling with contacts they had set up a meeting with who turned out to be three extra large men passable as Japanese Sumo wrestlers; also in tow, the minibus driver picking us up at the aerodrome. They huddled together in a corner of the saloon bar. We waited for them to finish their business. Eventually we spilled out of the establishment tanked up to the hilt. It was close to seven before we climbed back into the people carrier to return to Manston. With no immediate remedy on hand for Steve's verbal diarrhoea we had to harden ourselves to his haranguing us about how much this trip cost him. Ranking material wealth as more important than life, he was agitato over minor financial losses that day: until he levelled out I thought a tranquilliser injection might be on the cards to slow him down before his heart burst out of his chest Alien style. The word rant summed up Steve that day more than previously and might have been designed for him alone had he not been born long after it was first thought of. He kept shouting at the boys that he didn't see why they had to eat half the cows in Kent in one day and drink the pub dry at his expense.

"Ain't none of you got any money? What do you think I am?"

Steve didn't give me any hassle although I was answerable for committing him to pay an outrageous amount of cash to settle our bill. What made it harder for him was he didn't get a pork scratching out of that restaurant. Without considering the budgetary implications of following his advice to go and sort the food and drink then he would settle the damage later, I decided to invite his minions to do the same when actually he meant just me. At fifteen quid a steak, not to mention the bottles of whisky at bar prices me and my impromptu party happily consumed for a few hours, Steve was hundreds down as it was all added to his slate.

He was complaining en route to the aerodrome. I don't remember either taking off or the flight back, having given way to alcohol. Awoken by juddering on touchdown at Prestwick, my need to sleep hadn't been satisfied. Steve was still furious, though with longer pauses between each tirade. Deciding to shut the noise out, dozing for most of the car journey back to Hamilton Road was my sole response. We got there about midnight.

I left Glasgow early the next morning because I had to earn money. The eventual long nap the previous day had been fortunate as I was fresh to drive to Aberdeen.

That trip to Kent was one of many absurd things I did during my confused stage. There I was with a partner and children in Essex, touring the United Kingdom without them knowing, acting like some irresponsible teenager.

Steve's day trips were how he made his living. He had a lot to do with the haulage business and was always negotiating terms with the corrupt who arranged the transportation and dispatch of various merchandise. Everything was a commodity to Steve; he would have sold air if possible. He had this agreement with somebody in London relieving companies of their consignments on a road somewhere. There could be a phone call one evening and the next day his lorry unit would be mobilised. Sending a couple of his boys out to do the heavy stuff, he would usually see them return with booty that had to be got rid of quickly.

Gold was his favourite; it could be turned rapidly into cash: chains, earrings, rings, watches. If you wanted gold Steve could get it for you. The logistics of his operations were complicated, an intelligence behind them all co-ordinated from his head. Unlike the rest of us he had no need for a filing system. He had his lackeys make up sets of items in medium size leather containers for contacts to sell all over Scotland. They would buy the cases from him then go off and make whatever profit they could out of each sale that happened mainly in pubs and clubs. Drink, clothes, leather jackets, nothing was out of the question if it could be turned into money with the least possible risk of being traced back to him. Usually, I couldn't make a genuine driving error without being stopped by the police, yet here was a man who crossed the finest of fine lines between legal and illegal practices on a regular basis and got away with it. He justified his business methods by saying he was doing the mugs a favour by selling them expensive goods at knock down prices; it cost him next to nothing to obtain those items.

Over the five year period between 1991 and 1996 I found myself involved in many other mad projects masterminded by Steve. As I was living in Essex Doug used to fly down to a small airfield in Stebbing located on the A120 between Dunmow and Braintree. It was about half an hour from my home. That was how I was able to lie to Jackie about where I was without arousing her suspicion. I would park my motor and within three hours be sitting in a room in Glasgow having a cup of tea. Due to the inconsistent availability of the plane, I drove to Scotland many more times than I flew although with the speed I went through my impatience to get there - always watching out for police on my tail - when I arrived I felt as if I had flown. Irregularly, Steve would travel down with Doug. Doug would meet me and with his cheeky Irish grin and a wit to match tell me he had brought "the old cocker". It made Steve sound like he was Doug's pet spaniel when in fact Doug's term of endearment was a reference to his boss having cockney roots.

I got stranded once. We flew to Prestwick, landed, and I did my stuff in Glasgow. The following day we returned to Prestwick where we were told the aircraft was in the hangar undergoing repairs. I was supposed to be home that night as I had an impending conference with this oil company. A further complication was that I had not finished essential reports for the meeting. When I finally got hold of Steve he sent one of his boys over to pick me up from the airport then drive me to Essex. Joining my vehicle at Stebbing aerodrome got me home with about four hours to spare before the event was due to start.

Chapter Thirteen

The slightest effort and I was exhausted. I would habitually spend the night downstairs sprawled across the couch. In the couple of weeks running up to one of the worst facets of this affair it seemed as if I had barely half a day's sleep altogether. On waking from recurring dreams of throwing my family into poverty, the fear of making the break to do what I had to was overwhelming.

Jackie would never accept who I really was. Her company and our offsprings' energy and laughter keeping the house alive would all be lost to me. Either I remained, became a glorified lodger and stayed economically comfortable but unhappy, or left so that Jackie would be free to find someone who would love her the way she wanted to be. At least if I went the children stood a better chance of growing up in a stable home.

In the past I have pushed the theory that my suffering - indeed the agony of everyone diagnosed with gender dysphoria - can be traced back to a genetic defect. Resigning myself to the fact I wrongly accepted this as the sole origin of that hell - perhaps because it didn't make me feel so accountable for the trail of destruction I had left behind me - has been a real lesson in humility. Making such an adamant sweeping statement about how I was a poor, confused person who nature had punished shows how desperate I was. Gender dysphoria may have many causes none of which are proven: there is no black and white answer as to what creates the dissonance; possibly several factors come together to make it happen. More research is vital to test the genetic defect theory, among others.

What if I wanted to attend dance or keep fit classes? A penis and a leotard don't go together. That thing dangling down there stopped me from living. Before I had gender realignment I was convinced that once the male genital organ was removed I would consider myself close enough to being a woman for my gender dysphoria to disappear leaving me in a state of bliss. I knew I could still have problems; the major exertion over, with female bits my transition almost complete, I could have a go at tackling the daily round as a woman. The excess baggage had to be removed. It didn't function. The medication shrank it.

I can sit back now and discuss this openly because I'm more grown up about it. I'm so laid back, I'm dangerous. Then, with my depression the way it was, I could have hacked the lot off and bled to death.

Realising that old man love muscle would help construct the sensitive parts of my vagina, particularly my clitoris, I had to admit the appendage wasting away down there had its uses. All that told the world I was masculine had to go and soon would: the male member was only a temporary inconvenience.

Steve had started bringing me clothes that tacky transvestite strippers and kiss-a-grams would have refused to wear in public. He wanted me to look stupid enough to entertain his friends: a sort of "Here comes the dumb blonde transvestite, game for a laugh and the odd STD if he's unlucky."

He insisted that whatever I thought I owned belonged to him. I had never heard him talk like that before. The clothes I wore were mine. I had bought them with my money. He told me he had loaned them to me.

Once in 1994, while on one of my working holidays north of the border - as up until then visiting Steve had always been a holiday - I dropped in to see him. Craig treated me to one of his bear hugs which was like I had been clamped in a giant vice with cushioned jaws. I would enjoy it in my girlie way even if I was risking cracked ribs. I hadn't intended to stay there that night. One thing led to more than another. There were seven of us in the house. We all ended up having a drink; several drinks. In the end, the drinks had me. Out of those seven, that included me, I knew Steve, Ewan, and Craig. I had never set eyes on the other three before and I wouldn't want to again without the cover of a police marksman. There was a definite evil about them; they looked like they were about to kill and that was when they were buoyant. They drank furiously from bottles clenched in their rough male hands. I imagined the stuff they were swigging trickling down their gullets, blending with the slime and gastric juices in their stomachs. The hate inside them was the nearest they had to a soul that like a wasp sting only a thousandfold worse would be injected into some unfortunate victim.

It really does my head in, this. I cringe at the thought of reliving an episode I still can't believe Steve allowed to happen. I trusted him to protect me. It is part of my story and if I censor it I am breaking my commitment to getting as close to the truth about myself as I can.

I had driven for most of the day and I felt tired. That, plus the drink - which I knew I should not have had - set the agenda for trouble. Once again I became the actor, ironically, playing Steve's favourite gay male transvestite, more false than my much hated ordinary male role, catapulted bleary-eyed into a seedy world. This was nothing to do with being girlie. I take full blame for my stupidity in allowing myself to become vulnerable. Talked into slipping into what I would wear for Steve on a normal visit, I walked on to a stage where the audience included three strange men who would have looked at home in a boxing ring. When I had changed I remember Steve saying: "That feels better, doesn't it?" Here I became a sad parody of femininity in a tacky burlesque where I was mocked with each turn. I was the entertainment for the rest of the evening.

However much I drank that night I am certain it wasn't enough to make me semi-comatose. I am sure somebody spiked my drinks. I was spiked in another way too, or that is what it felt like. I passed out. The next eight hours were dreadful.

On waking, I thought I was in bed with my partner. I turned over to find one of Steve's unknown guests stirring beside me. My underwear had been removed. I was only wearing the dress I had on for that humiliating soirée. Inflammation in my rectum caused me to reach down and check the area concerned. It was slightly wet to touch. Palpitations in my chest through my heartbeat quickening with the distress over what damage might have occurred meant I had to put greater effort into controlling my breathing to slow them down. I stared at my fingers. There was blood on them. This cut-throat lying next to me heaved himself out of the bed and left without a word. A sharp, thrusting pain was fresh in my memory, the residue of its cause still attached to me like some parasite. The worst thing that could have happened to me, short of murder, had. Once the bleeding stopped and the soreness eased it should have been all right; after going to the toilet there was more blood. A fullness in my stomach with a colicky pain gradually replaced the original symptoms, lasting on and off for days. I started to think it was delayed shock, possibly a psychosomatic reaction to the assault.

Shouting at someone, at anyone, to tell me it hadn't happened, the effort of it beyond what I thought I was capable of, overstrung, confused, like a helpless child abandoned by friends, that place took on the shape of hell. Steve and Ewan knew I wasn't gay and didn't want any part of that world. I had always made that clear. For a while I could think of nothing else. As far as my feelings for Steve were concerned, I hadn't any.

Craig was an ex-marine. He knew how to deal with dissenters who upset Steve. The brute fact was if you didn't return what was Steve's to order you would wish you had never borrowed it. He was judge and jury. I think he identified strongly with the Krays and may have fantasised he was one of them. From when we lost contact around the late nineteen sixties, give or take a year or two, he had developed a social network that protected him. For about a quarter of a century he had lived off this, surfing on his popularity with other people who thought the same way.

By that point Jackie and I were on different paths with ambitions totally opposed to one another. I had to tell her what happened in Glasgow. It took me ages to do this. I kept going upstairs and sitting on the edge of the bed fretting over how I would break it to her. She asked me repeatedly what was wrong with me and this drove me to give her a frank answer. Pushed too far one day I came right out with it: "I've been raped," I yelled, silver stars in my eyes I had shouted so loud. The first thing she asked me once

I had made the revelation was: "Did you go to the police about it?"
I told her it had happened about twelve to eighteen months earlier.

"I hope you haven't given me AIDS," she shrieked.

"You know I wouldn't have risked your life like that," I assured
her. "I had tests done at Harley Street."

"Harley Street? How much did that cost?"

Waiting for the outcome of those tests was agony. The worry
of that alone left me psychologically and physically useless. For a
while I had little more than the confidence of a small, frightened
child. The results arrived and I was given the all clear for any
sexually transmitted disease.

Telling Jackie about the rape brought terrible consequences.
We were still lying in the same bed, but we weren't having sex any
more. In her eyes our sexual relationship, driven by her, once
contaminated by me destroyed our ability to be physically close to
each other. There was no more touching and kissing. The mutual
trust we had was gone.

Chapter Fourteen

The start of spring 1995 saw Steve becoming increasingly restless. Suddenly the house in Hamilton Road was no longer big enough for him. He had noticed one for sale he liked that was nearer the city centre. With a large price tag on it, the mansion he referred to had all the comforts he craved. He used to talk about that place as if it was already his.

One night we were sitting down having a drink when Steve pressurised me to invest in his proposed new home. "Didn't you ruddy well hear?" he challenged in cross-examination mode, irritated by my silence. "When we get possession we can share it. It'll pay off."

His idea was that he would sell the present asset which was apparently half Ewan's then whatever I could come up with together with the rest would make the asking price. Explaining to Steve I was saving money for my future, highlighting I couldn't use any of that to contribute towards his house purchase, was my way of being up front with him. I already had a home in Essex. Those trips to Scotland were an added bonus, or had been before the rape. I wouldn't need them after my gender realignment. My words died on me. He treated them with contempt because they expressed a view that got in the way of his plans.

"A short term loan then?" he suggested, this option less complicated, as he put it. Bells should have rang then. Steve didn't need money from me or Ewan. According to his endless rants over the years, bragging about how much he owned, he already had enough to buy the property himself. When I mentioned this he came back with the excuse that all his dough was tied up in an important project. Advising him that he could take out a mortgage given that the lavish abode he had must have been worth a fortune, I put it to him that surely this would go half way towards what he required.

"We don't want a mortgage," snarled his expletive loaded answer.

Idle chatter wasn't Steve's style. He was only interested in his palace, warning us we would regret it if we didn't go through with the deal. At the beginning of August he changed tack, giving us an ultimatum: "Make your minds up fast or you're out."

Facing Steve head on, more forcefully than I had ever been with him, I said: "Look, you know how important the money I have is to me. I don't want to tie that up in real estate."

He waited a moment before responding. "All I'm asking you is to give me a bit of financial support. Come on, you old queen. I'll make it right with you."

I might have been listening with caution but the klaxons were still not sounding loudly enough.

"I've got someone for this," he went on. "Part of the money's already here."

Before, Steve had said I could transfer my contribution by banker's draft which was useful for larger purchases and relatively secure because only the named payee can use the cheque. Once I agreed to the dubious arrangement I wouldn't listen to my intuition telling me not to be stupid.

Unable to sleep for the next couple of days because the money issue kept niggling at me, I had to check with Steve that everything was all right. That little bit of cash as he called it was my fortune. It would have provided the safety net necessary to carry on having a reasonable standard of living as well as pay for my operation. Looking back, I appreciate how I got my priorities wrong, putting my interests above the welfare of my loved ones.

The fact I was unwell is no mitigation for failing to take care of my partner, my children, and the rest of my family, including my mum and dad.

Dashing around, struggling to maintain self-control, lost in turmoil that aggravated my nervous energy, I tried to get Steve on his mobile.

The Tuesday following the bank holiday, Ewan sent me an urgent request to meet him.

Imagining all sorts of tragedies as possible reasons for his desperation to speak to me in person, I couldn't understand why initially Ewan wouldn't tell me what was wrong. All the way up to Glasgow I kept ringing Steve. His phone was turned off. There were several moments when I should have been intercepted by the police the speeds I was doing up the M6. My poor car barely stopped until I got to Hamilton Road some six hours later. Pulling up a couple of feet from the front door of the residency, I was greeted by Ewan. My temper had been building up during my drive north. Seeing Ewan in a dither caused me to shout. His face was white. I thought he was going to need a blood transfusion on the spot.

"What's the matter, Ewan?"

"You'd better come in," he mumbled. "You're about to look as sick as me."

"Had a commercial rival hurt Steve?" I asked myself.

"What is it, Ewan? Has Steve had an accident?"

Starting to shake, a wave of disgust rolling through me, I went hot then cold. My sickness at Steve's betrayal of our trust went deep inside me. It felt as though I had been struck instantly by a virus that left me temporarily helpless.

"He's cheated us, hasn't he?" I roared at Ewan.

Ewan fielded my anger by dropping his hesitant behaviour to give me the truth straight up.

"It's worse than that," he revealed. "He's done a runner."

"With our money?" I heard myself yell to the entertainment of the neighbours who found it impossible to mind their own business.

"There was no purchase made either by Steve or on his behalf, but there's been a sale all right: this house. He's sold it behind our backs."

Over a stiff drink Ewan explained how Steve had not returned from a trip to the city the day after I last saw him.

"I looked for his passport and it's gone. I've asked all the boys and no one of late has reported any sighting of him and Craig. Steve requested they stay away until today, then I took a call for him this morning from a person demanding we cleared and vacated here, handing in the keys by Thursday as they had a client coming up from Brighton on Friday. When I asked the caller what he was going on about he dropped the proverbial bombshell."

"Have you contacted the police yet?" was one of my first pieces of useless advice in reaction to the worst news of the century.

"How could he sell this without you being involved? That's stupid," I continued. "I'm not on the deeds," came Ewan's pathetic answer. "Why the hell didn't you tell me you were nothing more than a lodger?" I raged, my voice going into its unwelcome deeper male sound. I had the bank on the blower and while hollering at Ewan I put up with being told by some woman that I had to consult a member of staff there in person to get my account details. Giving Ewan the ear bashing of his life, my voice still raised, I reasoned that Steve wouldn't do this to us because apart from Craig, who was really only his favourite fancy henchman, we were all he had. Slamming the receiver down, I regathered my energy and drove to the source of my discontent like a formula one champion let loose around Monaco in a high performance vehicle.

The stereotypical male bank manager was direct and clinical. Even though he wore a name badge, from my point of view he was just another man in a suit. He said money had been transferred from my account according to my instructions. Well and truly up himself, the bank manager saw me leave his room in a fury that turned him girlie for a few seconds before he reclaimed his authority as male chauvinist executive. I was surprised by my intensity when I charged out of the building, threw myself back in the car and hit the gas.

To this day I have heard nothing more from Steve. He killed our relationship including happy memories we shared. Ewan and I hired a private detective to find him. He was traced to Canada. We couldn't take the investigation further because he had virtually bankrupted us.

This loss had a serious effect on the cash flow situation of my company. Things started to get hard after that. The firm I used to do most of my work for went into receivership. Despite the fact I was broke, the dreadful events of the previous couple of weeks motivated me to get my life back in order. Steve had been manipulating me on and off for eight years. Now I was going to run my own show without the interference I had put up with from some people for too long.

Chapter Fifteen

With three children you can find yourself seeking the advice of your doctor regularly. We built a positive relationship with our GP. He treated us as equals and would ask me things like: "How's mum?", meaning Jackie's mum, then would want to know how Jackie and the children were. I felt I could approach him on any problem we had no matter how terrible it was, except my gender dysphoria. My dilemma over whether to come out or keep my real identity hidden sent me into a tailspin. I thought: "What's the matter with me? Why don't I tell him?" I knew that all doctors are bound by a strict code of ethics that includes patient confidentiality but I found it as hard to make such a disclosure to him as I did my mum.

He gave me prescriptions for all these tablets I didn't want: analgesics for headaches, sleeping pills for insomnia and anti-depressants for depression. It took me several visits to tell him what I had to have.

"I need hormones," I insisted.

He said he couldn't give me that sort of medication. Hormones could only be prescribed by a psychiatrist. Yet more delays. Unless I wanted to take the unhappy step of obtaining them from the black market that without medical supervision would have left me exposed to the risk of being ripped off or killed, my only choice was to go through the proper channels.

On my doctor's advice I contacted the Albany and told health care professionals there my problem. It was agreed that I visited the top notch organisation one day the following week to go over all the treatment options open to me. No longer a patient of the clinic because I had nearly run out of money, by only paying their advice fees and for essential additions - initially a blood test result to be sent to my doctor - it was still possible to get help there until I received my first appointment at Charing Cross. As ever, the staff were supportive.

I had a bi-monthly guidance session that cost seventy to eighty pounds. When I began consultations at Charing Cross the experts took control. They decided the advice the Albany gave me didn't count. A psychiatrist criticised the decision to refer me to that establishment. With equal bluntness I maintained that my physician hadn't assigned me to this wonderful private clinic. It had been my choice to go there. From my point of view I assisted my doctor: through my attending the Albany he could get what I understood to be a bona fide medical report on my state of health, and progress, if any, which wasn't at the expense of the NHS. The psychiatrist was totally unsympathetic and told me in a strong voice like that of my old headmaster: "When you come here you'll do what I say."

Later, in the midst of a programme of treatment, he warned me he was going to take me off the hormones he had eventually prescribed me. I lost my temper.

"Not a very feminine way to behave," he scoffed. That phrase springs to mind when I am at my lowest ebb; it galls me. I remember how that kind of interaction made me over defensive. My memory of being patronised there in spite of my usually assertive personality still gnaws away at me. His was a stereotypical male view of what is and isn't the right way for a woman to conduct herself. I abhorred his sexist slant. Whatever the reasons were for this aggressive interview style, a large number of women taken off any street in the country would have objected to being spoken to like that.

Trying to get my head around why I did what I did to Jackie was like struggling to solve a crossword puzzle with cryptic clues. It was my wanting to be like her that made it possible for me to love and deceive her at the same time. She had a presence that set off extreme thoughts and emotions in me. Had I been born a biological female I believe Jackie and I would have still been drawn to each other and become close without any sexual involvement between us to ruin our friendship. In my dreams we would have been two straight girls who chatted together nonstop sharing the intimate details of our lives, being there for each other.

Like with Tammie Martin in my school days, my view of Jackie wasn't a realistic one: my idea of her as the kind of woman I wanted to be on the outside, while staying me on the inside, differed from how she saw herself. When I met her I had more or less convinced myself I would never be allowed to become a woman. That is why I had to keep promoting a masculine appearance.

I didn't just mentally switch on the male role though. When I first saw Jackie in that pub, here and there the conflicts inside me might have caused me to respond to her as a straight male would towards a straight female. Chatting her up was, as far as I remember, a natural, spontaneous move for me. I didn't fake it. The few episodes it did surface, "attracted male seeks attractive female" didn't last. It was a mood I would succumb to for an hour or so: I can only describe it as going upstairs with my male head on, then, to shake off the depression, having to come down as myself.

My identification with Jackie was based on fantasy. Wanting to be similar to her as I saw her drove me every day. I married her because I loved her as the person I imagined she was. Categorically I don't want this to read as if I didn't think Jackie was sexually attractive. Her allure was unquestionable. I didn't lust after her: I felt we had this bond without sex getting in the way.

What we had at the start was enough for me to feel close to her. Another contradictory bit of me is that I have never been what I call a tactile person. If Jackie wanted me to cuddle her I would do it but not without her asking me first. Some instances when we were sitting on the couch together during one of her passionate clinches I would get this incredible warmth pass through me. Like with the cuddles, if Jackie wanted sex I would oblige if I could: I would never volunteer.

I believe I made the most of the situation knowing that as long as I couldn't be a woman, and more to the point, a woman like her, at least I could have her near me and that in my mind was love.

I had been giving my future some thought, analysing our marital failure.

Doubting I would meet a man with whom I could have a full romantic and sexual involvement may have seemed overly pessimistic. Realism drove me to take this sceptical view: I didn't expect it because I was aware that whoever I got involved with would have to accept my condition, think for themselves, and be practical. Admittedly that was a tall order. I am not waiting on anyone. That doesn't mean I wouldn't do things for my other half. An equal partnership essential, my spouse would need the self-awareness and maturity to cope with the baggage that came with me. My earlier statement was arrogant. I know without the slightest hint of doubt I would never put up with being downtrodden. If that amounts to my expectations being too high then I probably won't end up with anyone because I am not going to change. My ability to fend for myself and low tolerance of people who can't look after themselves within reason would rule out any man who thought I should be there to attend his every need twenty-four seven. He would be waiting forever. Whoever had a close liaison with me expecting all the problems we had to be sorted by me wouldn't last five minutes.

In my male existence sex was either bottom of my agenda or right off it. My hope was that it would be top after everything that needed doing had been done. That hasn't happened yet. I have always preferred to think of myself as having a loving relationship without sex. Once I admitted this to my partner she got angry because sex was important to her: she couldn't fathom how I talked about intimacy without mentioning it. Male-to-female transsexuals in a male and female relationship tend to have a low sex drive. Ordinarily I had the libido of a corpse that had been warmed up. When I did achieve an erection I had a problem keeping it up. My head was telling me: "No. This is a possessive love, which isn't love at all. I want to lose myself in her, yet I have to be really pushed to get even a little way towards meeting her physical needs. It's not right."

She was the image of my ideal self. I screened out any details that threatened to spoil this.

I imagined myself into the sex act with her. In my distorted world I was always being made love to. I encouraged her to be on top. Jackie was the most beautiful woman any man could have wanted. I confessed to her I had been selfish, that I still loved her, and the moment she felt she had to find another partner I would leave because I wanted her to have what she desired, which I was no longer able to give her. Really, I couldn't bear the idea of her getting ready to go out to meet a man while I was still on the scene. The thought of another person touching her, however innocent it was, made me jealous.

If Steve and I had slept together following my operation, because I finally possessed the right bits it would have been physically heterosexual. Steve was biased though and no matter how proficiently I adjusted my body to make it female he would always pigeonhole me as a gay male transvestite. Whatever I did at the height of my confusion was wrong, but in terms of social labels I was not homosexual and I hated being called transsexual despite having used the term sometimes in this book for the sake of clarity; how discombobulated I was. I can visualise a psychiatrist puzzling him or herself to death over this. I am enough to blow the national grid let alone the minds of those who look at gender identity in a simplistic way.

Psyching myself up for the coital side of lovemaking took some doing. "I've got to have sex with her," I thought when she said: "Let's go to bed." Nevertheless, I enjoyed the physical closeness and grew to love our cuddles. Jackie would always have to initiate one between us: once my barrier came down that warmth - like a tremendous electricity conducting through me making me fragile as if I was in the early stages of drunkenness - ended in me feeling protective of her and comforted by her. I watched her beautiful femininity flower and grow towards maturity, guiding the outward development of my own inner femaleness, and I could have loved her in a sisterly way free of any sexual obligation.

When I used the phrase possessive love I meant that I wanted her all to myself as she existed in my head. She needed me to love her like any husband would in a happy couple. My way and hers didn't go together. Our marriage was doomed.

Chapter Sixteen

Roughly a year before I left home Jackie stumbled across my secret. It was common practice in our household that if my car was available she would use it. Scratching around for clues as to what I was up to she found my appointment card for the Albany. I now realise that subconsciously I wanted her to know the truth; I had left it for her to find. Having already told her I was attending a clinic that dealt with alcoholism, at first I used this to explain what she had discovered. She was already many steps ahead of me. The card had a picture of a fairy in its top right hand corner. It was like one for a boutique or somewhere really girlie. Jackie had to investigate. She rang the number printed on it and got through to the Albany.

"Is this a clinic for people with alcohol problems?" she asked the girl on the other end of the phone who replied: "No. It's a gender clinic." Quoting the male name I was known as, Jackie asked if I was a patient there. The girl told her she couldn't give her that information and neither could any other member of staff. She did, however, go into great detail about the activities and goals of their business.

When I got home I felt as if I had walked into a tornado. Jackie and I had a dreadful row that lasted three hours. Unloading the full strength of her feelings on me, she then walked out of the house and about a hundred yards up the road to confide in her best friend.

That altercation saw every destructive emotion going exchanged between us. I still think about it today. On the one hand I was glad it was out in the open, on the other there was this sense of our unity having been destroyed. She kept shouting at me to tell her it wasn't true then asked me why I was doing this to her and the children. I wanted to hold her, she needed answers. She was laying out the precise details of what I had done over the years that hadn't added up on her emotional balance sheet. The shouting became screaming. As far as she was concerned, there was no money because I was spending it all on my perversion. I tried to give her honest answers to her questions. Her short breaks of calmness brought her no peace. There would be a few quieter moments then another explosion. I was telling the truth and it hurt the person closest to me to a greater extent than if I had carried on lying to her. As we sat down and discussed the crisis, I noticed her eyes. They stared coldly into mine, like they were just seeing me, tolerating me because I had information she wanted.

This lasted several months then Jackie seemed to mellow. For a short time family life ran smoothly except for brief eruptions between us. On the whole, it appeared that Jackie was trying to understand what was happening to me. During our easier moments I told her how I felt and why I acted the way I did. It looked to me as if the bond formed between us in the days when we first went out had rekindled, touching me at a deep level. With hindsight, I now know this wasn't real.

Several visits to my doctor, a few to the NHS clinic, and I was still kept off my medication. Trying to stay calm was an effort that failed, marked by the return of old tensions. My life started to revert to how it was before I went to the Albany. There would be the odd stiffy in the morning which was inconvenient and in a way surreal as if it was saying to me: "You can't get rid of me that quick." It reared its ugly head giving me temporary penile dementia.

Shaving was probably the activity I hated most about that phase, frequently ridding myself of what were not soft, girlie wisps, but rough, prickly male bristles popping out of my face and chin as well as from under my nose like they were made from strands of coconut hair.

I thought I could go to my doctor, tell him the mess I was in, he would say: "No problem," and carry on prescribing what I requested. That, of course, was another of my fantasies. Whatever I might have thought of the medical profession back then, I must admit that my GP, Doctor Smalley of Harlow, was marvellous. He put himself out to help me regardless of the fact I had caused him mega stress. The poor man was having to swot up on gender dysphoria and the effects of hormone therapy because he had never come across a patient like me in his entire career. Doctor Smalley managed to refer me to Doctor Dein at Charing Cross who had dealt with people carrying this burden.

When I sat in front of Doctor Dein, who was a top consultant at Saint Margaret's Hospital in Harlow, he asked me: "Do the children know what's happening to you?" and I had to say no. He said: "They should be told." Doctor Dein recommended that Jackie had a chat with him accompanied by me to try to help her understand gender dysphoria.

Undeniably, I was envious of Jackie's femininity. Now I was able to tell her how nice I thought she dressed, praising her impecc-able taste. To be able to talk about underwear, make-up, shoes, the works simply as two women who were friends at last brought out the better side of me again. I found I could still be sensitive and loving. During our chats I learned that Jackie didn't have any trendy skirts or a smart suit to wear. There was me happily going on about what I kept in storage, when she broke down in an upsetting show of tears. I had been so into my own universe I hadn't thought to ask her if she wanted any nice clothes. She and I impulse buying together was another change. I showed genuine interest in what she bought which pleased her for the wrong reasons. My latest problem was the effort to contain myself in that situation. Formerly, if my partner asked me to go shopping with her, nine times out of ten I would say no. On the odd occasions we did retail therapy as a couple we would descend on boutiques and outfitters more than any other type of shop. She always insisted I purchased clobber that suited me from her point of view, strictly for blokes, of course. My male wardrobe was the most pathetic display of uncool gear imaginable. You could have kept it in a few plastic bags from the local supermarket. An articulated lorry was needed to move my collection of female apparel down from Scotland.

Jackie and I agreed that the children were far too young to cope with the shock of me coming out: by keeping this from them we avoided a lot of extra tension. I think they would have been bullied at school and probably in the general neighbourhood as well. I did not want to increase the risk of that happening.

Our financial problems had to be solved. I have already mentioned the enormous debts. We decided I would stay for as long as it took me to pay those off.

Jackie gained strength from within to cope with the challenges that lay ahead of her. I learned from her. As I got worse, I watched her change into a strong, confident woman. From then on, her priority was to focus on what was right for her.

Towards the end, I sat around and couldn't be bothered with anything really. The mortgage had to be paid. I was still working, though nowhere near as much as I had been. That was because I didn't require the high income necessary to live a double existence any more.

One day, before Steve disappeared, possibly forever, Jackie criticised the friendship I had with him during an argument in which she stripped it of anything good it had ever meant to me. She sussed I was meeting other people on a more intimate level than business. Given that she knew my secret there was no longer any point in me keeping quiet about Steve.

"Any normal person being showered with the gifts you've been given would have suspected if not known there was an ulterior motive behind it," was the gist of her argument. "Nobody gives anybody anything for nothing," she lectured.

To allow Jackie some privacy I took off to Scotland for a few days. I had dramatic mood swings: one minute I would be all right, the next lose it. The situation at home had become sensitive to the point where even when I was calm I couldn't move without annoying her. From the moment she found out about Scotland, she continually cross-examined me. That put me on edge all the while, shortening my temper so much it would go off over as little as an innocent remark taken the wrong way. I had to give her a complete timetable of my recent and immediate future activities. She wouldn't tell me anything about herself though.

It became my priority to try to cushion my family from the inevitable break up that was coming. What increased the chances of further rows between Jackie and I was the fact I had been off my medication for a while and consequently taken over by those blasted male hormones.

I still wanted Jackie. In the early days of our marriage she put a huge effort into our sexual relationship. She had enough libido for both of us. Always beautiful, tactile, passionate, her sensual nature moved her to respond keenly to the mildest affectionate hint or touch from me.

We tried to talk about who I was and she kept accusing me of recklessly splitting up our family. That made me shout at her: "I'm not making a choice. I'm already this. You're looking at the real me."

Jackie said my decision would be the ultimate selfish act towards her and our children. She asked me why if I had managed to control *it*[1] - as she called my condition - for all the years I had known her, I couldn't stay as I was. All I loved about my life up until then was about to be lost.

She didn't know if she would ever tell the children who I really was: it could be too traumatic for them whatever the circumstances.

For years Jackie had done the accounts side of my business. She never once asked for a penny. There was a time when I believed she would always help me if I needed her. It got to a point where I could no longer guarantee this. Her friends were eroding whatever patience with me she had left.

No amount of self-awareness on my part could override the destructive forces in me that I took out on Jackie. Additional hardship for her came with her dad's tragic death. Quite apart from her anguish over his sudden dramatic passing, she was trying to look after her mum, deal with me, be a mother to our children, not to mention keep her career going.

I barely existed, going to work and accomplishing next to nothing else, perpetually tired because I wasn't sleeping properly. Jackie was having the same problem. The fact we knew we were both constantly exhausted didn't do anything to improve our relationship. We became less tolerant of each other. When we were in the same room together the vibe would be so bad one of us would have to leave. A difficult path to tread, the psychological and practical effects of her dad's demise caused the rift between us to widen. The end of our marriage was inevitable.

During a rare moment together Jackie asked me: "If there was this fit man and sexy woman standing side by side who would you pick?"

There wasn't a sexual thought in my head then, the energy that would have been my libido used to satisfy the only ambition I had which was to sort myself out. She persisted with her attempt to overcome my silence: "Surely if you want to be what you say you are you'd pick the man?" she queried. That was when I had to accentuate, however ridiculous it sounded to her, that sex wasn't important to me. I didn't know this hypothetical man or woman. Why should I pick either? I wanted her. Finding I couldn't handle any more disagreements, I capitulated. I wish I could have said I would have preferred the man but Jackie would have taken it to mean I was gay.

Note

1 Jackie referred to my way of being as *it* or *what* I really was, rather than *who* I really was.

Chapter Seventeen

Jackie told me I treated her and the children badly. I had become self-centred, using the bottle to escape my inadequacy, and I desperately wanted it to be true that my gender dysphoria was caused solely by a genetic defect. Even if that was the case it doesn't alter the fact I still had the freewill to make the choices I did. I chose to lie to Jackie. At least, despite what I believe to be a number of different elements influencing my destiny - including biological factors - I eventually tried to improve my circumstances.

My attempt at making the situation better began with my decision to continue medical intervention that would include surgery.

Forty-five years old, unable to follow a clear path, I wasn't going to the Albany then because I had promised my partner I wouldn't continue the gender realignment process until I had paid off my bills. My worry here was that the director of the clinic would say: "If you're not a regular patient then you're on your own." That would have meant waiting ages for an appointment at Charing Cross.

As stated earlier, there are legal changes that can be made to documents such as driving licences, those concerned with all personal insurance and tax, and passports. A usually straightforward particular on a certificate or permit, for example, can cause real problems for a person who has gender dysphoria.[1]

Identity and affiliation snags of one sort or another kept coming up. At the time of writing this, after gender realignment you couldn't marry in your proper role or if you were in a new relationship adopt any children related to you or your partner.

In 2004 the Gender Recognition Panel (GRP) was set up to alleviate these difficulties.

Sufferers of gender dysphoria are still perceived by those who do not understand it as sick individuals having their precious bodies tampered with, leading to the mistaken belief they cannot function adequately. For me, it was more irresponsible to go through life as I was, not caring about anyone other than myself. I walked around the house full of anger.

You can learn a lot about individuals through how they present. Socially effective attire need not be set to a rigid standard. If a woman displays clothes that taken as a whole are compatible with what is generally accepted as an appropriate way for males to dress, that doesn't necessarily mean she is saying: "I want to be male."

Are the psychiatrists really thinking: "How can you want to be a woman if you don't live in frilly dresses, sport bouffant hairstyles and use bright red nail varnish?" If some of them genuinely believe women don't normally wear trousers they can't be from this planet.

I accept that the decision to allow a person to have gender realignment surgery has to be made carefully. By watching the behaviour of individuals who claim to require this help over years rather than months a psychiatrist can judge how serious they are about living in the role of the sex they wish to be recognised as. People who know their bodies look and feel wrong genuinely want to put this right by having their shape, size, and detail adjusted to fit their beliefs about who they are.

We usually have to follow basic social values and norms that help us tell males from females. I wasn't going to adopt a stereotypical female dress code for the sake of looking girlie. Trousers were right for me as long as they were women's - which the ones I used definitely were - so what was the problem? I had been watching my partner. As a modern woman Jackie knew how to project herself. In a total of twenty-one days she donned a skirt twice, with tights and a nice top. Otherwise her style was casual: ski-pants, leggings, and jeans with a jumper and boots. She often didn't want to put on a frock, paint her nails red, or show off high-heeled shoes. With the wildest imagination you could never accuse Jackie of not looking feminine. Smart and caring about the way she appeared to herself and others, she expressed her femininity in a suitable way for each occasion both naturally and uniquely.

Today, re-examining what I wrote at that late stage of our dying marriage, I can appreciate how I would allow no one to trick me into believing I was not Carol Royce.

Livid and protesting: "I can't say I'm someone else any more to make this life my detractors want me to live work," they told me: "You're male - get on with it." I would sooner die than accept that.

A strong sense of sadness would cause me temporary loss of concentration. I had grown accustomed to my vitality ebbing away during intense moments with Jackie when I revealed my deeper emotions. Memories of my partner, children and me happy together were too much. I would walk out of the living room into the kitchen and light a calming cigarette before going to bed to finish working through my feelings.

I love my partner and my children. Jackie should never have been dragged into my life. I could have seen all this coming: if I had thought about it properly and been careful how I approached everything it would have been obvious there was a real danger that even if I innocently fantasised about being a woman the themes and issues of my youth would return.

It hurt me when we were all in the same room together and my children went straight to Jackie, clinging to her when they could have come and sat with me. All positive communication between us had been destroyed. Not privy to the kind of details that couples in happy relationships tell each other, no matter how trivial they are, family activities passed me by.

Jackie kept digging at me to answer her questions. I wanted to talk to her about clothes, make-up, and how we both felt. She said I was perverted. Sapped of energy I spoke her language to get through to her; I had to say I was guilty.

It was awkward at home and at work. I couldn't carry on with the job I did. Right from the moment I knew I was eligible for gender realignment surgery sooner rather than later, I eased off on the amount of manual activity I did for the business while stepping up my contribution to the office side of it. If I wasn't out there doing it myself though it was never done right. I tried taking on assistants. That failed expectations. To return permanently to how I was - constantly switching between the male persona and Carol - would have upset the psychiatrists. I saw myself spending the rest of my days worrying about having to explain why I was impersonating a female if I was caught out of male role. The company employed me because of my expertise which I had built up over the years; if the board knew I was staying in the office rather than going out to do the hands-on duties and the reason for this, the business would have suffered.

Maybe I was wrong to try to deal with my constraint single-handedly. I wouldn't recommend this to anyone except those of the strongest character. Some individuals would want as much support as they could get, eager to mix with not only those diagnosed with gender dysphoria, but others on a regular basis too.

A culture where it is easier for gender dysphorics to blend with the wider society as valued individuals would be a dream come true. I am not saying that being in a group where each member suffered from the same problem is not a positive step to becoming whole. It is nice to have someone who is going through exactly the same as you offer words of comfort. The odd bit of constructive criticism by telling a person they are not doing something right could be helpful without destroying their self-esteem.

Since the fallout Jackie and I hadn't stopped scrutinising our relationship. It felt like every sentence spoken in the whole of our married life was being slowly and viciously dissected.

One dream I hung on to until the last minutes of us as a couple was that after I had left Jackie would still be my friend. As I had created most of her problems I wanted to support her in her future attempts to solve them.

In the late summer of 1995 I returned to Scotland. My room had been emptied. All I could find of my stuff was a pair of earrings and a bracelet I ended up giving to Jackie. I had to reassure her I bought them for her. Knowing she liked those items of jewellery would have meant a lot. A few pounds worth of gold wasn't going to help her come to terms with who I was. If she did decide to wear them I wanted it to be special for her. Through little flashes of sentimentality now and then I wished she would get back in touch with the happier memories of our conjugal journey.

Towards the end Jackie would check up on me and find I was in Manchester when I should have been in Liverpool. At first it was easier to go back to lying, then, one day, I realised it wasn't even worth doing that any more. Ironically, when I told the truth she wouldn't believe a single word of it. "You're a liar," she would say to me. I think she was gathering as much evidence for her case as she could.

Note

1 See Chapter 10 for my account of a particular experience I had of this.

Chapter Eighteen

July 1996, Jackie, the children and I parted company. Sick with anxiety over what might happen to us all, I found it difficult to summon up the energy to pack. It was hard stopping myself from saying goodbye. Jackie and I stayed with the decision that it was for the best.

I am not blaming Jackie for anything. It was all my fault. I am responsible for what went wrong. Jackie had nothing to do with it.

She was determined our kids would never know who I really was. Gradually, she became quiet and distant.

That pivotal morning, with unbearable sorrow, I watched my brood leave the house to go to school. My throat tightened. I kept swallowing hard to relieve the aching fullness there: pain working its way out of me - anger and sadness that had built-up over the years, the last bit expelled in a pitiful scene marking the break up of my family. Like I had gone back to being an infant, I cried, the final sobs ending the release of this tension. The tears mildly stinging my eyes, all that was left of my hope for a reconciliation with Jackie which I had been clinging to dripped pathetically on to my bags like a few miserable raindrops shortly to evaporate. We had been together for twenty years. Once Jackie had departed with my little loved ones I loaded my cases into the car then left. I haven't seen them since.

Eyes closed, randomly sticking a pin in a map was how I chose where to go. It went through Cromer in Norfolk; this was to be the extraordinary location of my new start.

From 1993 until about the beginning of June or July 1996 I was on and off hormone therapy. Summer lightened my arrival in Cromer. When I got there the pace shocked me. It was bordering on dead stop.

I wasn't used to waiting ages for a bus. The shops in the town were small. Where I came from they were huge: about twenty-seven aisles. I went to Safeway in Cromer, had to queue about half an hour to buy food, would get angry, then leave the trolley behind and walk out.

The inhabitants on a mission to delay me, I stepped briskly along the pavement, a local yokel blocking it ahead talking to another. They would have died first had I not asked them to get out of my way. Some folk don't notice anything vital to their safety. This was the wrong season of the year to turn up there: if I had arrived in the winter when there were fewer bodies around I could have got my shopping done sooner by practising dodging the natives who were in a trance, then by the summer I would have been trained to deal with them and the dozy holidaymakers. Why don't people look where they are going? "Are they on something?" I asked myself: "How do I cope in a place like this where motion is slowed down to such a degree it is almost freeze-frame?" Life itself was on hold. I have got over that now.

Being without money and a roof over my head were my biggest concerns. I had been used to having most things; poverty came as a big shock, which is an understatement. Up until then I never had to worry about whether I had enough for a packet of cigarettes, a tank full of petrol, or my car tax, insurance and so on. It is like somebody asking you to give up smoking. You get anxious. The not knowing how to occupy yourself and the realisation that even if you did you wouldn't have the cash to make it worthwhile was about the size of it. Having to pay an amount of rent for your room that ate up most of what you got for your fortnightly social security benefit meant you spent all day there getting bored.

I was trapped. Sleeping in the afternoon helped to fill the long days. I felt as if I was in prison and wanted to escape. When the black thoughts and the confusion were bad I couldn't move.

Kindness was shown towards me over the weekend that followed, which I appreciated. I got on well with another person diagnosed with gender dysphoria whom I met at a party in Norwich run by two friends, Steph and Maxine. Her name was Nicky.

Nicky was from Cromer. I felt relaxed with her and the party's hosts, convinced that at last I had found companions who didn't want anything from me. Nicky, my first buddy after separating from my family, showed me what I thought was genuine friendship; a timely relief from physical, emotional and social shutdown. Here, I was able to retreat from the advancing ranks of insanity.

A force to contend with, I imagined Nicky and I taking on the world. We sat for hours going over any subject we could think of from cooking to what we wanted out of life. As I saw her in those first days of living with her, Nicky's finest quality was that she was a person who cared about others. When I looked back over the previous few months to consider what I had achieved, which was nothing, and then at what I had coped with in the week I met Nicky, I realised I had changed from being the defensive, depressed prima donna with barely more substance than my shadow when I walked into Steph and Maxine's house, to the self-assured person who believed she had a way out of her problems. There was the joy of having the choice to live again and it was exciting. I belonged here. Having waited forty-five years for fate to be on my side I wasn't going to let it slip away.

We had a girlie night out. An arrangement was made to pick up Steph and Maxine on the way to a special social event for those with gender identity issues. The highlight of the evening was the car journey there and back. While this may appear insensitive to those who enjoyed the gathering, from my point of view a lot of the individuals present were not really what we, or should I say I, was about. Certain what I can only call exhibitionists there irked me yet I tried to mix across the board: I felt compassion for some and wanted to help them, but that do wasn't for me. Resented by the show-offs monopolising this affair, who treated it like a fancy dress party, I knew I wouldn't make it to the end. Keeping to their side of the room, these overdressed drama queens glared at me as if I hadn't the right to breathe the same air. I made it clear I didn't like their attitude, upsetting their play acting that they appeared to be doing for cheap thrills. Where was the subtlety in their choice of clothes or the dignity in their behaviour? Why didn't they dress the way I thought females liked to for a night out instead of going to extremes? Organised professionally and responsibly with the best of intentions, it was a successful do for those it suited.

My alliance with Nicky was short-lived for unbeknown to me she was suffering from clinical depression. She became ill. During August 1996 I moved out of her house. Finding a note asking me to leave wasn't easy to take. With hindsight, too many difficulties complicated our pact. There were several years between us - not that an age gap should stop anybody being friends - though a young mind versus an older one is a well-known potential cause of friction. My laid back approach to practicalities was impossible for her to accept. In her mind issues affecting her required urgent attention. I couldn't stand it. We clashed. Having problems getting my benefit, the reason for which only the Department of Health and Social Security could throw light upon, meant I was unable to pay her rent for the first six weeks. That didn't help.

I found myself homeless. On the plus side I still had my car; at least I didn't have to sleep on the beach. Following about an hour of sitting in it parked by the sea front, I presented myself at the North Norfolk District Council office on the Holt road. Another long wait and a customer service administrator told me to go back where I had come from as there was no legal obligation to house me in this county. Pleading with them I was desperate for local lodgings because I no longer had a place to live in Essex and that they must know of at least one vacancy, they came up with details of an organisation for the homeless called Saint Matthew Housing. An appointment was made for me to have an interview there.

Darkness fell and it rained heavily, high winds sounding like I was in a storm in the middle of the north sea keeping me awake.

Unsettling me with their doleful moans, those gales tipped my emotional balance; this was my winter in the height of summer. What tiny slivers of confidence I had would be lost for several seconds then come back.

I had rather it hadn't; the next morning came and I faced a dilemma. Did I go as Carol or Ray? I chose Ray as legally that was who I was. I had not yet officially changed my name.

Saint Matthew's in Cromer was made-up of three houses. Arriving at the one where I was to have the meeting ten minutes before my appointment was a sign of my desperation to grab any scrap of certainty. Knowing I would at least get a roof over my head was a start. Had I been whole I would have arrived at any event with barely a minute to spare, loving the back against the wall feel of that. As it was, my misgivings about what I was doing, where I was going and the need to be careful over what I said and did ruined my natural spontaneity. Spending the early hours trying to sleep in my car wearing what for me were androgynous clothes, in a lay-by displaying a 'no overnight parking' sign (I still took some risks) because I didn't have much petrol and had no money, was uncomfortable. Aware of the slightest weird noise in the eerie spaces between the cries of each squall, I was worried the police would find me and ask me to move on. The clothes: pink shirt, jeans, and flip flops, that were all I had, I wore at the interview as Ray. If I had gone as Carol Royce I would have had no chance of getting accommodation because I didn't have any valid documents to hand to support the fact that Carol existed. My hair was a disaster, that and my hazardously long fingernails making me look like a super nance. A short while passed before this lady appeared and announced that her name was Moira. Straight away she reminded me of a nun. She was short, I suppose no taller than five feet. Her soothing smile was a relief to me. Moira was the house manager of a part of this set up. She interviewed me. One of those helpful people who inspired confidence in you however physically and emotionally battered you were, the way I felt, a halo above her head would not have gone amiss.

She showed me into her office, at all other times the kitchen, encouraging me to talk about myself which isn't always a bright idea depending on who you are. It was more of a chat than an interview. During our hour together Moira told me I would also have to be evaluated by a lady called Sheena who wouldn't be able to see me until that afternoon. Asked to come back at two, which I did, I repeated my story to Sheena, an outgoing and approachable woman whom I liked a lot. It was agreed that I could move into one of the hostels immediately. To begin with I had a room at the top. The house was big, my apartment on the fourth floor the size of a garden shed with barely enough space for a single bed and a wardrobe. Luckily, I was only in there for a week as I took over one occupied by a girl who had moved to the ground floor.

In those days of nowhere to run from myself - which was in bits with no manual to help me put it back together - despair was often turned into creativity. I wrote down particulars about my life: critical incidents that described the horror and the funny side of being human.

On day one I was properly introduced and taken to the sitting room. Two brothers whom I hadn't met on my first tour were swearing at each other. The moment I came in they stopped, looking at me as if their brains were telling them: "This does not compute." Both giants, they were well over six feet, Stewart the shorter of the two, Wayne at least three inches taller. They were covered in tattoos, the bits of their bodies still untouched by the needle likely to be filled with more words and pictures of death and decay, advice from Satan and other voices from the dark side unless they kept taking their medication. Any references to God would be added for the wrong reasons. Those two lads had to take prescription drugs that would knock an elephant out. Their smiles lacked a certain human quality. Starting a conversation with them wasn't as difficult as I had expected. Wayne offered me a cigarette that I took out of fear. I hadn't had one for yonks. I was shaking while they tried to spark the end. The heat coming from two igniters full on plus my nervousness made it the most dangerous light up of my life. That night, I smoked about twenty fags with my new friends who were seasoned nicotine addicts.

You didn't have to be a doctor to know Stewart and Wayne were unwell. Revolving their wrists or bouncing their legs up and down fast as if they were using a foot pump, ash falling on the floor from the glowing ends of their roll ups held precariously between their quivering brown fingers, it was clear those two needed help. Schizophrenia and manic depression stopped them from reaching the point where they could be ordinary young men.

When an individual appears threatening we usually think and act in ways that help us protect ourselves.

Even if there is no obvious risk to our safety, can we always suspend our judgement of a person - an evaluation based on knowledge, possibly incomplete, of the condition they have been diagnosed with - in our first meeting with the reality of their way of being as it unfolds before us?

Anyone who stands out because they appear strange and fail to function adequately can be valued and appreciated simply for their humanness.

Stewart and Wayne blamed their dad for the state they were in: hating both parents one minute, more dad than mum, the next high over the news the former was coming to see them, which was a rare event (in the almost two years I patronised Saint Matthew's, Cromer, I think he visited them twice), it was difficult to keep track of their constantly changing attitudes towards the two people who brought them into this world. As I got to know the brothers, they became calmer in my company. Once I had listened to their whinging about what was troubling them there would be these moments of comfortable silence between the three of us when I could temporarily forget they were unwell and touch on their humanness.

Sleep was something I had built-up a resistance to, the overstimulation of fellow residents coming back and forth to see me, filling my room and me with their largely negative emotions, turning me into a night owl with attitude.

Painfully early the following morning, concerned over having to tell somebody about my background, taking this to Sheena who was in the kitchen getting breakfast seemed the only way to end this pretence in order to be accepted by my fellow residents. Although I wasn't able to reveal then what I had held back in conversations with Moira and her, I made Sheena aware there was more to me than I had let on. Sheena slotted me into her diary for us to have a chat about what was really happening for me.

Traipsing to the Jobcentre to sort my housing benefit was more urgent than coming out to Sheena with the awkward truth that was my life. Otherwise, I would not have been able to have stayed at the hostel, the weekly rent punishing to an unemployed person.

I came back from the Jobcentre armed with my B1 that Sheena helped me fill in for my assessment. From there, disappearing to my room to write my letter to her, I was all day and most of the night trying to express the awkwardness of my predicament, not to mention how I would break it to her the person she thought I was didn't exist, followed by the jolt that I was gender dysphoric. Pleased I had managed to condense my life so that it fitted on two sheets of A4, the second read through still looked as if I was saying sorry.

Why did I have to change back into what I hated to be accepted? Sheena was marvellous. She said to me that when she first interviewed me she thought I was gay or an artist. That was all right. When I wasn't me I gave off confusing signals. I might as well have been me as the openness of the majority there made it pointless being otherwise.

The three Saint Matthew's houses were home to a diverse bunch of characters all with their own stories. I had this idea of their life streams trickling into mine and I realised how we can all connect as human beings whatever our individual differences.

At the first of these the eldest was a lovable man called Walter. He had the nickname 'the eating machine'.

Jessie, then twenty-two, suffered from a bulimic type disorder. She weighed at least twenty stone. Between them both, Jessie and Walter could empty a well-stocked fridge in a day.

Kelly had an acute problem with one of her legs which was swollen with fluid. She also had cerebral palsy.

Gavin, arguably the least troubled of all the residents living at Saint Matthew's then, was the only one in the house who worked. He used to do long hours at the Cromer crab factory. The hardest person to talk to until I won his trust, he did have a refreshing realist streak.

"If you want to be Carol, I like Carol, no problem," he reassured me after a tedious session explaining to him all the inroads and cul de sacs of what it was like to be me. Sadly, Gavin left the house a few months later.

Moving from the primary set of digs to the secondary was funny. During the week before I left house number one the residents of my new address had all discussed whether I should be allowed to move in with them. My reputation for being strong-willed and argumentative followed me wherever I went. Arriving with a bang, I tried to be fair from the start of my tenure right through to the end. By confronting most of the other residents hiding in the kitchen before I put my belongings down I stopped the place from turning into a social wasteland. I could hear voices - not in my head yet, though I was getting close to it - coming from behind the kitchen door, some slightly raised, others giggling like infants. Those of them who could string a sentence together were talking about me as if I was being tried without jury. The silence I got when I opened the kitchen door was like the whole world had shutdown for two minutes.

"I'm here. You know all about me. If you don't like it I've been told to tell you that you can leave because I'm staying. Any questions?" I lectured, then a consoling grin spread across my face relieving it of the tension gripping it before I broke their cycle of whinging and piss taking, I picked up my stuff and asked to be shown to my room.

The second Saint Matthew's lodging I lived in was next door to house number one. It had a couple of self-contained flats on two floors. Many small rooms were furnished. There was a large communal kitchen in both premises which the occupants shared, taking it in turns to cook for one another. Each side had a lounge that was arranged nicely.

A lot of friendships I formed in those houses continued after I had left. One of these was with Damon Albarn not to be mistaken for the lead singer of the nineties pop group Blur although this has happened more than once with hilarious consequences. His birth name was Gary. He was being called this when he first set foot in a Saint Matthew's hostel. Damon was a young man of twenty-one the day Sheena brought him to live at the house where I was. His life up to then had been an emotional minefield. Confusion and misery filled his days. I worried about him as if I was his mum. Years later he still gave me cause for concern. Damon looked at the floor a lot when he tried to talk. He found it difficult to make eye contact. His energy stemmed from nervousness and might have explained why I had seen more meat on a rasher of bacon than his body. I discovered he had a thyroid problem. Vastly improved since our first meeting through gradually coming out of his shell, nowadays he has his own flat in North Walsham.

Leon, a guy we all found difficult to accept, moved into house number two with me. This young man took a lot of understanding. If we were Venus he was definitely Mars. He had been hit on the head with a baseball bat. According to unconfirmed reports from less than reliable sources, a metal plate was fitted over his skull to stop it caving in. Most of the other residents called him metal head. As cruel as this was he took it well. One of my temporarily adopted sons, I loved him. His manic disposition hard to keep up with - always haring about with nothing definite to aim for - in the end he had to go somewhere.

The day Leon arrived he stank. Living on the beach, he certainly didn't smell of Chanel number five. He reeked of rotting fish, seaweed, body odour and tents. The ducking he needed was along the lines of a sheep dip, followed by a tub of hot water, carbolic soap, vigorous scrubbing then a cold shower to be on the safe side. Unfortunately, he didn't agree. His smell got everywhere. When I was first near him I gave a controlled retch to ease the rolling ache in my throat that spread to my stomach. I wasn't there to do his washing for him and tell him when to have a bath. At least he was happy. I admired his ability to keep his past separate from his present. No one ever found out about Leon's family. He wouldn't talk about his mum and dad. All we knew was he came from Norwich.

Gerald had the air and behaviour of a slightly upgraded tramp living on bacon sandwiches and toast, shuffling about holding a mobile phone. He was another person who found it hard to have a wash. Gerald's signature was his long, greasy hair and dirty, untidy appearance. His clothes looked as if they wanted prising off him. Either they would eventually rot away or have to be surgically removed he had used them so long. He wore his jacket in the hottest weather, walking around Cromer with his toes poking out of his shoes. There was no need for him to do this because he had money put away, but he didn't like spending it. What happened to Gerald was sad too. Having worked in the kitchen of a Norfolk school for most of his life he had never got over being sacked from that job for allegedly ignoring some health and safety rules. It was because he was uneducated that he had little or no chance of securing gainful employment in the future.

The lovable JT was another of my surrogate sons. A young man in his thirties unfortunate enough to have learning difficulties, John Thomas was vulnerable to exploitation from other boys in the house. That is why I took care of him. Committed to stopping this slow, pleasant, always zealous to please gentle giant from being used, I befriended him. I showed him kindness which I don't think he'd had much of. He became emotionally attached to me; he got confused, believing we were man and wife.

Coming to in the early hours of one memorable morning was fortunate because it gave me time to react. An orange glow radiating from an outside light filtered through the darkness. It gently touched the walls and the chaotic ruffle of my bedclothes, my groggy, half aware state pushing toward full alertness. Like the morning after in a film or television programme, my vision slowly phased into focus to behold this large male appendage both in length and girth, dangling in front of my face, apparently talking to me. Surely I heard it mumbling, its words spoken in a deep, stretched out voice, delayed, slowed down to near stationary, begging: "Carol, will you sleep with me? I'll wear my pants in bed." It was JT, bless. While most people I knew spoke at forty-five revolutions per minute JT was a forty-five rpm record playing at thirty-three and a third.

Pulling myself up, swinging round with a force and speed that surpassed my usual reflexes, my discovery that this whopping great phallus was attached to JT didn't make the situation any less disturbing. Throwing him his dressing gown, relieved that he was already putting his pants back on which he must have either had in his hand or nearby, saw me telling him straight up that we couldn't be together like this. Once I had settled him he sat on the edge of my bed and agreed that a passionate affair between us would be impractical, not to mention disastrous.

JT had told his mum about my condition using words like: "Carol used to be a man" and when this woman dropped in on him she treated me as if I was sad and pitiable. Though I was glad I had eased JT's own struggle at the house by befriending and protecting him, to me it felt like his mum was only sympathetic towards me because I had done this. I didn't require her sympathy. Acceptance was what I needed and I seriously wondered whether she would have given me either if I had not watched over JT.

The public eye saw JT as a child in an adult body. Everybody at the house liked him. Blissfully unaware of what was happening in the real world, he had an exceptional gift: he could remember almost any pop record released between the mid-1950s and mid-1990s and tell you the name of the artist who recorded it, the song title, and the highest position it reached in the charts.

Residents there were, in the main, mentally children, yet physically adults with sex drives to match. If I encouraged JT to help me in the kitchen he would think it was a come on. What I want to remember, besides the fun and the jokes, that I hope can be seen as affectionate in JT's case because from my point of view they were, is his innocence. Corruption hadn't got to him and I don't think it ever will. Strip away the politically correct label 'intellectually challenged' that had been slapped on him and you had a human being who was simply nice whenever he was in your company.

A boarder called Martin was deeply depressed. If he didn't like you he would let you know. He had worked at the school where Gerald Bean was employed but he left due to ill health. We discovered that Gerald and Martin were brought up together in the same institution. Martin was a clean person, always in the bath. He seemed infatuated with me, his affection expressed through buying me stuff, usually junk. I had so much clutter dumped on me made up of unwanted gifts I was running out of space, nearly having to take on another room for storage. He loved my cooking. They say: "The way to a man's heart is through his stomach", except I didn't want to get to his heart by any route, least of all his stomach. In sympathy with Martin too, I wished to show him a bit of kindness to help him on his way. When I left he broke down. I did go back to see him and he had improved.

Nineteen year old Josh was someone else looking for maternal love. He would never talk about his parents. A smart young man wearing designer clothes that he got out of all the people he knew, who were mainly from London, he looked seriously out of place in that hostel. It struck me that Josh was troubled about his sexuality. He tried to prove he was a man, not an easy goal to achieve for a mixed up young male. Also running against him was the block he had with girls that caused him to treat them like dirt. I asked him if he was gay. He said no. Although he surrounded himself with women he appeared to be happier in male company. His need to control both sexes echoed throughout our family, as I liked to call it. Josh ended up in Florida with a male partner who owned a bar and night club.

Taylor, who like Josh was smart and about nineteen when we met, already lived in the house before I moved in. He was sitting in the kitchen. Before we opened our mouths we hit it off - what you might call instant rapport. We fascinated each other. One of those guys I felt I had known for ages, I was comfortable with Taylor and my first words to him were: "You're definitely gay." He was frank, which helped me. That made it all right for me to talk openly. Previously, I had not discussed my circumstances and history with any of the residents in those two houses, only Moira and Sheena. Taylor and I would recall our childhoods, part of the effect of ending up poor and having to live in a hostel for the homeless.

Damon had this weird idea of hanging my teddy bear, Ted. When Ted got to fifty I stuck a badge on him that said: "I am fifty and loaded." He was a symbol of my childhood. Still having the original bit of ribbon around his neck, evidently I had cared for him. Damon and Taylor decided that Ted was suicidal through spending too many years with me. From their point of view it was kinder to put him out of his misery. An ultimatum was given to me in the form of a ransom note warning me that if I didn't stop nagging them I would never see my Ted alive again. What went through my mind was that I'd had that Teddy all those years then two young men still wet behind the ears come along all set to destroy him. They did have the decency to bury him in a plastic bag. Damon explained: "We treated him with a bit of respect giving him a cross and a funeral service that Carol failed to attend."

I didn't even know about the funeral.

Taylor is still a friend, occasionally phoning me for a whinge as well as to make sure I am all right, in that order.

Patrick shouted. One of two residents who worked in the house, it had gone around Cromer he was a pervert. He might as well have worn a bright red t-shirt with the word printed on it in large, black lettering. The trouble he found himself in started before I arrived. It goes without saying that I don't tolerate child molesters. I had no idea whether he was guilty of this allegation; I refused to judge him over it. Patrick reminds me of how difficult it is to view individuals simply as ways of being without wanting to give them a label. He pushed me to the limit. I had to confront him. Shouting at me in his girlie voice, which you could barely tell apart from that of the average female, he got an unwanted surprise. I pushed him into the kitchen with me and slammed the door behind us in one great dam burst of energy. At a volume louder than his, I warned him to back off. The look on his face was one of shock. He was a child in a strong, male way with a girlie voice that didn't match. Some will say I am being unfair. They don't know how much that bloke asked for it by the way he wound me and the other residents up and interfered in our lives. He made me feel I should apologise for being gender dysphoric.

If it doesn't encroach on other people's space or put them in danger, haven't I the right to be who I really am? Hasn't anybody who follows this general principle?

It could be argued that when certain folk don't understand a person's potentially discrediting difference from others, however that shows itself, they may fear it, and that might cause them to dislike and consequently want to harm the unfortunate individual. All right, but then if that, say, non-acceptance of me develops into verbal abuse or physical violence I have to defend myself to survive it. Isn't that the human instinct of self-preservation?

Patrick changed following my confrontation with him. Perhaps the incident increased the tolerance threshold we had set for each other?

Once I had shaken him up I had done my bit and left the room. Pat went from maniac to mouse. Everybody had been frightened of him. He never raised his voice to me again. Pat has visited me at my flat in North Walsham. If he treated me the same way he did at Cromer before our run in we would be sworn enemies. His voice is still irritatingly high, which I know he can't help and I have learned to tolerate; by the time he has gone though I have usually got a headache from it.

A second Martin, whom I saw little of, had one of the self-contained flats. When he did leave his pad he would come downstairs to talk to me about horse racing, a subject I knew nothing about. I once looked inside his living space. It was decorated in designer nicotine. The walls were yellow-brown caused by the tar from his full strength capstan cigarettes, also absorbed by furniture and carpets. You would be a passive smoker without him there simply by sitting in his flat on a hot day.

The next person I liked was Colin who was the house manager after Moira. Although Colin and I started off on the wrong foot because I had applied for the manager's job when Moira was leaving it and he never told me he was also up for the post, we too became friends. When he realised who had competed with him for the vacancy, he came over to console me, staying for about three hours.

I felt sorry for Jessie. We watched her make a sandwich once. It was a whole loaf and a block of cheese stacked on a plate. "It's only a cheese sandwich," she protested.

"That's not a sandwich," said Sheena. "That's a four course meal."

Sheena decided Jess should go to number twenty-six where she could fend for herself. We all had our own fridges with locks on them. The privileged had master keys; your food wasn't as safe as you thought. Jess charged me £7 for a dinner she cooked. It was spaghetti Bolognese. Just a few of us sat down to it. I was the only one expected to pay.

Damon would remark in her defence: "She does nice cakes."

The roast dinners were Tudor style banquets. This girl ate a five pound chicken that she tore to bits like Henry VIII. Twelve Aunt Bessie's Yorkshire puddings, two pans of roast potatoes, plus a whole cauliflower with the chicken ended in misery when during her struggle to digest all this her stomach would go into trauma. Despite the setbacks she suffered caused by her large form Jess was a lovely person. I remember her coming into my room as I was sorting my clothes to ask me if she could have one of my skirts. Given that I was a size twelve and she was a twenty-eight I nearly rolled off the bed swallowing the cigarette I was smoking. It was my black Lycra skirt she fancied.

"I'd like to think I could wear that one day," were her words, which made me sad. Wanting to offer her some hope, I let her have the skirt. She would hang it in a wardrobe and get it out to look at when she felt low. The girls and even some of the boys borrowed a lot of my clothes indefinitely. It was a wonder I came out of there with anything.

Teresa, walking around the house in bare feet, didn't have any shoes. I gave her a pair of mine I had bought but never used. They were brand new worth about £80 and she went out and wrecked them. She walked them straight through the mud down by the boating lake.

One day Steph and I gave her a makeover. It took us hours to turn her into an attractive young woman. Her boyfriend walked in, saw how nice she looked and ripped it all off of her. He wanted her to be scruffy because he could only feel at ease with her if she was like that. Before coming to the house Teresa and her boyfriend lived in Sheringham. There were so many bin bags in the flat they occupied, some full of maggots, they were evicted for being a public health hazard. In their eyes money came before safety. Teresa's boyfriend had taken all the lead off the roof of the building that housed their flat. He stripped the tiles from it and sold them. Open to the elements, the loft space filled with water and the ceiling collapsed. They were instantly homeless. It was this that brought them to the exotic location of Cromer.

When she was younger Teresa had been in a serious road accident. She was an adult child constantly grappling with her surroundings. Damon used to spot her walking around Sheringham.

"She looked as if she'd come out of a coal mine," he once recalled.

Teresa was on medication, her partner an alcoholic. Their

highly individual ways of being were to a large degree caused by the substances they took.

Steph and I were inseparable for a few months until Damon came into the equation. She used to say to me: "Do you like Damon? I really fancy him." I would reply: "If he oils your wheels and starts them turning, tell him", because I had the hots for Steph's on/off admirer, Zac, who might have been called Roll on/Roll off for reasons I am not going into. Most times when Steph was out of the way, distracted by the ever-confusing world of Damon, Zac used to visit my room and sit on the edge of my bed. He was ultra cuddly, confiding in me about Steph because he was gutted when she left him.

"I was probably the male slut of the house," Damon reflected, years afterwards.

I found it difficult to keep my Bohemian friend in particular away from my clothes and make up. When you spot a guy who is six feet four wearing a twelve inch Lycra skirt it is a sight you never forget. He had the skinniest pins I have seen in a pair of tights.

Chapter Nineteen

Over five hundred days passed while I was with Saint Matthew Housing. Initially the chaos was wonderful. My friends opened my eyes to a reality that had previously been my passing sorrow on seeing destitute souls wandering city streets: the teacher became the pupil.

During my stint at one address there was a huge turnover of residents. Several of those people's lives became part of my own. My dive looked like some old railway station waiting room. An alarm would go off regularly because there were many smokers puffing away in there. Occasionally it was that bad I couldn't see my hands in front of my face. I put a cover over the bed to tone down the stink of fags on the duvet. There were evenings when the fug hung around for hours causing me to have to open the patio doors to let the draught suck it out.

From where I am now it is clear to me that my stay in Cromer forced me to learn to do without things I had taken for granted. Living on next to nothing was a steep learning curve. All the lads in the house made sure I didn't want for much as far as cigarettes and wine were concerned. I soon knocked the joint into shape. One of the changes I made was to arrange a kitty for food. That meant we all ate well. The girls and boys who made up my team were unemployed. Money I used to collect from my magnificent eight amounted to £15 a week each, allowing me to get quite a stash to pay for the nutritional boost they deserved, plus a few luxuries. Beans on toast was strictly off the menu when I was in charge. Satisfaction at watching their lethargic behaviour and general lack of direction transformed into a healthier lifestyle improved the quality of my own. A structure to their day and the value I placed on them, which they could appreciate by the way I cared they ate properly and had order to their existences, helped.

To me, some of them were like tramps with no purpose, prepared to stay in bed until noon then get up to go to the off licence and squander their benefit there, or take drugs, sooner than pay the rent. I am not claiming I single-handedly changed their lives for the better.

Before my clamp down I was washing and ironing more than my fair share of clothes. Male hygiene was poor compared to the girls'. Not only was a lot of the boys' stuff offensive to my nostrils, they dumped their rank laundry in the washing machine without any powder, expecting it to miraculously come out clean.

From small beginnings I got a community going. My new kids on the block achieved an improved way of living through learning by example. In spite of their limited resources they became social rather than antisocial. Once trained to a basic level of responsibility awareness, they were motivated to help one another raise standards, sharing their know-how. Above all, they could solve their own problems because they thought in a more focused, adult way. In each case I didn't want to take away their individuality. It was more a matter of smoothing their rough edges to give them, and all of us for that matter, healthier, richer lives. Telling a twenty-seven year old to leave the toilet in a hygienic state after he had been is not information most mentors would imagine having to impart, but that is another example of what it was like. Of course, I was grateful the person actually used the toilet in the first place and not the garden. The next step was to encourage him to care enough to wipe the seat if he had peed on it, pull the chain, then wash his hands in the washbasin. Remember that most of these youngsters were ill-treated from an early age, kicked out to fend for themselves when they couldn't; they saw any demands made on them as unreasonable, retaliating by withdrawing or being aggressive.

I work on the belief that there is good in everyone. Ask someone to carry out a task instead of demand it and it will probably get done. When I was supervising the boys and girls at the second home I lived in I used to make sure they completed their share of the cleaning on our side of the house. The kitchen was my job because I was the one who used to do the cooking, with a little help from Damon. Spelling out to my team that domestic chores were necessary because if they were not sorted the premises would rapidly become a health hazard gave them a reason for co-operating. A community needs leadership and organisation plus a balance between authority and love.

Crucially, a bond of trust creating friendships was established with most of the residents there, evidenced by how today they take the trouble to travel from Cromer to North Walsham to visit me when they don't have to.

Staff at Unwin's off-licence knew us well for stocking up before our all night drinking parties full of bad behaviour including the X-rated humour when we relieved our stress through the most spontaneous and enjoyable of all therapies: laughter. The language hit a tone a tad blue during those crazy sessions of human contact and the group dynamics generated by them; it was living in the moment for the moment.

Frank first saw me in male mode. The second occasion I met him I was dressed as a female. No wonder the poor man couldn't figure out who I was. His friend Jim asked me in a less than subtle way: "Did you used to be a bloke?" which I ignored. He responded to my silence with a phrase that was as aggravating to me as being poked with a sharp object then having it corkscrewed into my skin.

"Are you a transvestite?"

"No," I said curtly.

"What other sort is there?"

This dumb conversation between us came up like indigestion at regular intervals over the next two years. On days when Frank and others wanted to know particulars about me they were straight to the point with their questions. They couldn't understand my replies. However much I tried to accept them for who they were, the temptation to label them ignorant was hard to resist.

During the early stage of my relocation to North Walsham, Frank graced me with his presence. Although he told me he liked the way I always gave him straightforward answers, my responses encouraged big debates that exhausted me with their repetition. Frank claimed he had served in the army. He talked about the SAS and if he ever was with them he was probably employed as a cook. His whole life centred around the tablets he took. He would reveal: "I've been to the doctor's. I'm on more pills," before he said hello. That was the gist of his mindset. He liked everyone to know he was ill. Frank would be on his way home then think about details he had forgotten to mention and have to wander all the way back to discuss them. He couldn't let anything go. Whatever played on his mind kept him awake until he had put it right. It takes some imagining guessing what he would have been like without his chronic anxiety that was eased by controlled medication given to him regularly by his Community Psychiatric Nurse. Sitting in my flat, arriving on a Friday, leaving on a Sunday afternoon, I used to let him vent his frustration. Frank would stand on my doorstep greeting me with those ominous words that told me he would be staying the weekend: "Can I have a bath, Carol?" Though I listened to him it was to show him acceptance and valuation. However, on another level, the impression that Frank was not a well man would never be far from my thoughts. His repetitive behaviour was, if nothing else, wasting his and everybody else's energy. When I was with him, as much as I tried not to, I could only perceive him as obsessive-compulsive to the point where it did my head in. Sadly, Frank is no longer with us.

Towards the end of my year at number twenty-six sadness was a part of my life again. In the two weeks prior to his death I had become close to a young man called Joe. Turning to drink with his friends, who were the drunks of Cromer, he found his way back to the downward spiral he had never really escaped. One of these sots used a syringe to inject himself in Joe's bedroom. Unfortunately, there was a random inspection of Joe's quarters and the instrument was found. The hostel staff who made the discovery assumed it was Joe's. Without any discussion sentence was passed on him. He was told to leave. Within a few days he was dead.

Keith, who was in his mid-fifties, was a problem at first. "I'm not calling you Carol. That's a girl's name," were the supportive words I got from him. I soon pulled this relationship into line. By the time I left, Keith happily addressed me as Carol and I got a kiss from him.

Regularly bleaching the work surface in the kitchen lacked the glamour I wanted in my life. For hygiene's sake I had to do this in order to keep at bay the salmonella, e-coli, or anything else nasty that was bound to hit us otherwise.

Sexy, with the loveliest black hair, dead straight, that went right down his back, perfect tanned skin as if he had just got off his horse in the Arizona desert, Richard was unique. Claiming one of his relations was a Sioux Indian, he exploited the assets nature had given him. Richard was such an English name for someone with alleged American Indian blood. I could see the Sioux in him. He only needed a horse, some war paint, and the picture would be complete.

Asking Richard not to mark a table top after I had polished it was an invitation for him to reveal his maverick streak by climbing onto said furniture for the sole purpose of winding me up. When I grabbed his feet he lost his balance and I watched the shock capture his face as he hit the floor. He was all right and laughed about it. That marked the beginning of our understanding of each other.

I remember the knees-up during the Cromer Carnival celebrations of 1997. Our inaugural planning day for the jamboree started like any other. First thing in the morning we all sat around a table smoking and drinking coffee, having a chat about what we were going to do over the next twenty-four hours. Earlier in the week the subject of the coming annual highlight of Cromer's social life was raised by one of the residents. "Why can't we have a float?" a voice queried. "What about the organisation involved with it?" I said. There was a short silence. "Let's do it," enthused Sheena. "It'll be fun."

A strategic plan was drawn up indicating who was appointed to do what. We would get hold of materials and try to con the blissfully ignorant into providing us with a suitable vehicle for the day. It was difficult imagining a respectable member of the public offering to lend one to a group of punters they didn't know who looked like a bunch of delinquents. Out came the yellow pages. It seemed hopeless then I dialled a magic number and a man with a polite tone answered. I went through my rehearsed patter expecting negativity and he told me to hang on while he found out if he had a spare truck that weekend. He was gone for about five minutes. During this interlude cheap sounding high street store music played distractingly in my ear. He came back on the line saying: "You're in luck."

I asked him what he would charge, explaining we were a charity that couldn't afford a lot. "You can use it if you have an HGV driver and can get him to drop in on us in the morning with his licence," was his welcome reply. As luck would have it Robert could drive a lorry. He agreed to go.

On the day, I spotted our float in the procession and shook my head; there they were, pale, lifeless ghosts on the back with Robert driving, looking like he had made the public relations mistake of his life. Big Wayne, dressed as the grim reaper, warmed up a bit, doing his version of robotic dancing to a trance soundtrack, part of which gave the impression he was having an epileptic fit. The transporter passed so slowly through the mass of happy people it was excruciating to watch. Each member of my little community had a mask on that was enough to terrify the children running around. They wore hooded capes made from old rummage sale clothes, the cardboard sickles they wielded unconvincing. The irony of it struck me. I wished to live and they all wanted to die.

December 1997 saw me experiencing symptoms that over several weeks made me think of giving up smoking. A circulation problem affecting one of my arms was the cause. On the wedding ring finger of my left hand an appearance began to concern me. Beginning as red dots under that nail and the ones either side of it, the doctor diagnosed Raynaud's disease. He prescribed drugs for this then asked me to call on him every week for about a month so he could monitor its progress. Growing worse, the pain made sure my nights were almost sleepless, spent largely pacing the floor holding my left hand under my right armpit. My finger looked as though it had been hit with a hammer. During the day I tried not to bang it doing what had to be done. All the doctor did was give me different tablets. Pills were not going to stop the drawing, knife sharp spasms. Swallowing alcohol to deaden their slow, stabbing rhythm, contained in black, swollen tissue dying on the end of my hand gave no lasting relief.

Snow fell and the rarity of a blizzard in Cromer amplified the misery.

Unable to take my glove off during an emergency visit to my doctor, he removed it for me, saw the seething flesh, picked up the telephone and called an ambulance. The drama had an imaginary romantic air to it, for I was whisked off to the Norfolk and Norwich Hospital where I was treated by a lovely physician called Doctor Clarke.

Every medic there except Doctor Clarke told me my bad finger had to come off. Keen to preserve my painfully embarrassing digit that resembled a feature of the male anatomy I could have easily done without, he vowed to try to save it. About two o'clock in the morning on or about the second day I was there I fancied a cup of tea. Venturing into the nurses' station one of them asked me: "Can we help you?" The only thing I could think of was to display my infected pointer in front of her bewildered face and say: "My hand has grown a penis." As I said this she spat her coffee across the room nearly showering her colleagues with it. Most of my life had been spent wanting to get rid of a penis and now I had one sprouting on my mitt, emerging from my transforming, inflamed protuberance to the point of having a hole on the top of it that was in the middle where dead tissue had fallen away, its helmet ending at the first joint.

The place was in uproar. That silly outburst on my part, pun intended, helped the week go by better than it would have done had I not got to know all those nurses, who used to drop by and check on how I was doing, guaranteed a dose of my humour to lighten a taxing day.

Doctor Clarke had a stock phrase when he arrived at my bedside on his morning ward round: "It might hurt but it's still there." Over the next week regular tests were done to analyse the state of my blood. Worried about the gangrene in my ailing extremity, Doctor Clarke kept his promise by saving it. It is still safely attached in as near to its original form as possible. Though more slender, it blends with the rest of my left hand.

If my understanding is correct, the tiny blood vessels at the end of it were blocked. Blood was unable to circulate there causing the existing tissue to die slowly. A surgical team was assigned to remove the blockage. On the fifth day, I went down to the operating theatre. The surgeons had to make a hole in one of my legs to allow a cannula to be inserted, going up the main artery to my heart. Anaesthetic was injected into the site. This only deadened that small area: I was able to feel much of what was being done. Like a worm wriggling up inside me, the sensation of the fibre optic camera heralded the start of about two and a half hours in theatre. The length of time under repair was necessary because they couldn't stop the bleeding where the device entered my body.

Warfarin is glorified rat poison. I had taken a lot of it over that week to thin my red stuff. The moment the tube was in position there was instant relief in my finger through getting a decent blood supply. It changed from black to pink, and with further treatment the poison cleared from my system.

One Friday during a visit to Cromer Jobcentre accompanied by a colleague who knew about my life because she had lived in a Saint Matthew's house with me, things turned bad.

Ahead of me in the queue, my acquaintance signed on, left the service point and waited outside. While I was still in the building she told this thug details about me I had disclosed to her in confidence. He had his small army of mates with him. When I came out of the Jobcentre they thought they would have a bit of fun winding me up, then give me a kicking.

Tired of Cromer, exhausted by the life I was living, I'd had enough of the house, its inhabitants, the works. I was going nowhere, like a robot, cooking, cleaning, and thinking for my charges twenty-four seven.

On leaving the Jobcentre, I was wired, overwrought, and consequently didn't register what that kid said to me. Whether I could hear him or not I knew by his attitude he was slagging me off. I hit him hard on the side of his head. He went down. It was one of those moments when I reacted badly, the situation becoming desperate with his mates standing around me, staring. Thug had lost his power. He looked defenceless, as if I had reduced him to the fragility of a small child. Blood was coming out of both his ears as well as his nose and mouth. Realising the state he was in, I panicked and ran from the scene.

Pushing past several bodies gathered there, I walked briskly back to the house and went straight to my room where I sat on my bed shaking. Supported by those present who wanted to know what was wrong - Colin, Sheena, and Moira in particular - I realised how genuine my little community was. Paranoid that the police were going to bang on the door and come in and arrest me for killing Thug, I stayed in my room. Regretting what I had done, fearing its consequences, I thought my life had stopped.

About an hour and a half had passed when the doorbell went. It was Jane, Thug's girlfriend. She had come to tell me he was all right. In spite of hearing that reassuring news I remained uneasy, failing to understand why I did it.

Sheena and the social worker told me I had to get out. Emotionally, the other residents were keeping me there. They were growing and I wasn't. Arriving as these poor, homeless, unwell victims, I directed them towards improving their social skills by teaching them to live and work together. In the end it was taking so much out of me I had nothing left for myself.

I went into those houses confused but still strong, a strength that was gradually whittled away by my fellow lodgers over a period of nearly two years. It took four weeks from when it was decided I should leave to get my flat in North Walsham. The help I got from Sheena, Julian Housing (that Sheena had started to work for full-time), and the social workers, was awesome.

One of the hardest steps I took was tell mum. I had not set eyes on her since I moved away in 1996. Before leaving Cromer I spoke to a clinical psychologist and in the usual frustrated manner tried to rationalise my world to him in the hour allowed for the appointment. He listened to me patiently then at the end of the session advised me to face what I had been avoiding.

"You need to contact your parents, especially your mum," he said.

Throughout the interview I kept mentioning my mum and the psychologist picked up on this.

"Why are you talking to me when you can chat with your mum?" he queried with a logic that caused me to think seriously.

He also reiterated the point that where I was based lacked the stimulation necessary for me to progress. Here was a medical professional who wanted me to develop in a way I felt positive about. I am grateful to that psychologist. Without him I would probably be stagnating, or dead.

Life dealt me some tough lessons at Cromer. Previously, my arrogance left no room for understanding folk less fortunate than me. My fellow inmates were down on their luck to such an extent, I was made to think. I found myself in a place I knew existed and would never have believed how bad it was until I was part of it. Unemployment wasn't new to me although I had never been out of work for long. Young boys and girls with mental illnesses that made them unpredictable were challenging. Those youngsters barely functioned. Out in the real world they were hopelessly lost which was why they ended up being looked after by Saint Matthew's.

Writing the following letter to mum brought back harsh memories of the upheaval of leaving home in July 1996. It also led to my reunion with Tracy.

"Dear Mum,

I'm sorry it has taken me so long to write and it doesn't seem as if I care about anyone but I do. I hope you and dad are well. This letter is my way of explaining why I left and also to say how much I love you both.

I suffer from a condition called gender dysphoria. I've known for most of my life that I've hated my male body. I was unhappy living as a man and wanted to be a woman. What with the effect it was having on me, and my concern for you, dad, my brothers, Jackie and my children, I had to go away.

Since I left I've changed my name and live totally as a female. I have a flat in Norfolk, help people instead of use them, and made true friends who accept me as I am. I know there are those who will find this hard to swallow. If you can handle it and meet me as I am please come and stay. I live in a small town called North Walsham. It's not far from the sea and I reckon you'll like it. If you're worried about what the curtain twitchers might think or say, don't be. They only know me as Carol Royce. I've spent nearly three years building my new life.

Please write to me mum.

Yours with love, Carol."

Being on my own in a rented apartment in rural Norfolk was still at odds with my outgoing personality. I wanted company. This became a craving that had to be satisfied. Growing curious over the comings and goings of the neighbourhood, I noticed things I would never have taken the slightest interest in before, believing this change was due to my inner self finding its way to the surface.

Chapter Twenty

When I arrived in North Walsham I decided to do something useful with my life. I chose voluntary work because I aimed to help people and promptly contacted Nina DuFeu. She was the co-ordinator for the North Walsham district of Norfolk Voluntary Services based at the town's cottage hospital. I spoke to her at length, telling her that if I was going to do this type of activity in an honest way, which was what I wanted, anyone I befriended must know the truth about me. In the autumn of 1998, Nina had a lady in mind she thought I would like to meet.

Diane was to be my first befriender. We both joined the scheme for the same reason. I made up my mind that once we met if Diane found my condition intolerable I would not contact her again: Nina had discussed this with both of us separately prior to the introduction. All went well. I hit it off with Diane straight away. She turned out to be refreshingly open-minded and talented.

Her husband Peter has a raft of admirable qualities. He is a kind soul who has time for everyone. A brilliant cook, Peter makes the best meat pies in Norfolk. His survival kits which are small bags of food that he gives me on most of my visits are typical of his generosity. For some years he worked hard for the Women's Institute Market that nowadays allows men to assist with that side of the organisation. His products became known to many of the older and some of the younger residents of the town: an example of postmodernism and cultural diversity (terms I have heard but still scratch my head over)?; one of my little in-jokes. The word postmodern fails to click with Peter. In his view a concept is either old or modern and I agree with him. An accomplished painter, a talent presently on hold, that and his practical skills come together to make him one of the most versatile individuals I have met.

In her younger days Diane was a successful performer with the Chelmsford and Witham amateur dramatic societies. She was involved mainly with the Chelmsford Operatic and Dramatic Society but also formerly a member of Witham Operatic and Dramatic Society and the Chelmsford Festival Players. In 1948 she was the youngest person ever in Chelmsford to be given the lead role in a production. It was a musical called "No, no, Nanette" and the shows took place at the Regent Theatre in the town. She was fifteen. Her reviews were excellent. I was impressed. Diane's other explorations into the arts include drawing, painting and poetry. I have read and would recommend a couple of slim volumes she has written and had published herself demonstrating her gift for producing a touching style of traditional poetry and prose.

David is a kind, gentle person who tries to understand all and sundry. It is an impossible task. Since I have been acquainted with him I have become more tolerant.

I have known Gail for several years. She has multiple sclerosis. Approachable, dedicated and selfless, she has supported me since I moved into my flat. Through her my eyes have been opened as to how I really feel about myself. I thought I was the most hard done by inhabitant of the estate until I met and befriended Gail. My problems were put into perspective when I saw the complications this poor woman had to endure. What she does for her friends and family is remarkable. With a genuine zest for life and plenty of drive she can stand up to any obstacle that stops her from progressing. I don't think she gets back the kindness she hands out. Gail doesn't give to receive. She appears to be in pain, yet it seems to me that some of her circle don't grasp the full implications of the disease disrupting her quality of life. It is how she battles on that I find inspiring: always venturing to do better. Gail is the sister I found in 1998.

We are both the same age, bar a few months, and have a marvellous rapport. Our lives have worked out similarly insofar as the choices we made: you know, been there the same, done that the same. Now we either can't find the t-shirts or their colours are faded and they don't wear too well. Marriage, kids, money, have all given us pain as well as pleasure. Our children have flitted in and out of our lives and occasionally, much to their inconvenience, found we haven't any money, while sometimes they have done well for themselves and made us proud.

Looking at us both together I am extrovert while Gail probably leans more towards the introverted side. We complement each other which makes our relationship balance well. Mum and dad have practically adopted Gail into our family.

Gail, Diane, Peter and David all treat me like a person. The medicalised process of gender realignment largely doesn't allow you to be one. That is certainly how I found it.

For consultants to recommend gender realignment surgery strict criteria for eligibility have to be met. Such a clinical approach potentially increases the likelihood of gender dysphorics being too concerned with what looks right and therefore reluctant to disclose details of their experiences that may help improve others' cognizance of their condition. As a result, they could become more alienated than if they had been open about what was happening to them, causing them to withdraw from the world.

I also argue that the confrontational interview style I had to put up with can do more harm than good to genuine sufferers of gender dysphoria. They are hurt and dismayed by the often total lack of comprehension out there. This journey cannot be made alone. Once diagnosed with a gender identity disorder I became a non-person: a label; I was classed as mentally ill. Trying to keep everything within the psychiatrists' prescribed schedule from initial diagnosis to surgery has led some in this predicament to become a tragic mess. They struggled following doctors' orders, which they had to honour to get to first base.

One consultant said to me: "What do you want to do this for? You're being selfish. You've got children. You should be thinking of them." I never stop considering my children. Most of this book is about me admitting my selfishness. I don't want a psychiatrist lecturing me on that issue. For years I tried to accept how I had been made. I started relationships, married and had kids. That led to all manner of problems including heavy financial losses and catastrophic emotional upheaval. I ruined my partners' and my children's lives.

A psychiatrist at Charing Cross told me I had to be gainfully employed and pass as a female before surgery was even a remote possibility. Convinced I couldn't wait for a full-time job and universal acceptance that I was female, I was close to turning in on myself and ending it all.

I felt I had to lie again; I had to trick society. To the psychiatrists it didn't count that I worked part-time as a volunteer for the Citizen's Advice Bureau. They wouldn't consider me for surgery unless I had been in a full-time paid occupation for at least a year.

Part-time voluntary work, which was what I did, used to be accepted: large numbers of the populace who are not gender dysphoric do this without any other job and are relatively content with their lot. For the Charing Cross psychiatrists it was only one step towards their definition of employment. My whole week had to be occupied by what they decided was useful activity.

Shortly before Christmas 1999, anticipating one of my last Monday training sessions to work as a voluntary adviser for the CAB, I was in Norwich strolling past City Hall that runs parallel to the market place when my shoulder was grabbed, pulling me round quickly with the force involved. Momentarily losing concentration, the world span for a few seconds before I realised my bag had been snatched by two young males who had already robbed an old pensioner of her Christmas gas bill money as she was getting off a bus. My emptied bag was lobbed onto one of the coloured awnings of the market stalls. A reasonably fit man walking behind me gave chase but couldn't catch up with them. Local news reports revealed that a gang was operating in Norwich targeting susceptible citizens. It must have been one of those rare cases I looked unprotected and got mugged.

Following that I remember telling my CAB supervisor at North Walsham: "They rob us then come here for our help. We give them information on how to get legal aid to defend themselves in court from being prosecuted for mugging us."

The thought of my supervisor sorting out my neighbour's objection to me complaining about him damaging my health with his lifestyle struck me as ridiculous until it actually happened.

Poking her head through the inner door to her interview room she had opened slightly to stop my dear neighbour watching me practise my customer service skills - trying to look happy and helpful which was false because I felt the exact opposite - my supervisor attempted to speak to me without him hearing, her face apologetic.

"There's a Mister Spring here wanting to know how to sue you," she whispered. I believed it was a barely audible voice in my head at first, me thinking: "To cap it all, I've gone schizophrenic."

If I'd had to sit there and deal with another person asking me how to get a passport, or demand the post office to refund the cost of a postage stamp that hadn't stuck on an envelope, I would have hit my final nervous breakdown. Virtually everybody I knew who lived on the same estate as me sussed I worked for the CAB. Some visited my flat to ask for advice on a variety of topics and issues. All that made me decide this wasn't for me. I wanted to help those struggling with real problems who put effort into changing their lives for the better without taking others' hard earned cash and property.

Told by the psychiatrists I wasn't sticking to the rules of the real life test, yet quite able and prepared to sit on the opposite side of a desk in the office of a voluntary organisation for no payment, I wondered if I could ever do anything right for anyone. Many who turned up at the CAB seeking guidance were unemployed with no prospects at all, having to look after large families. Were they behaving according to society's rules? At least they functioned. Given my circumstances, was the psychiatrists' definition of adhering to regulations reasonable? What did they expect of me? On a later visit, when I mentioned my voluntary work, one asked me: "What do you want to do that for? That doesn't bring any money in."

In my male role I had worked for years supporting a family, paying income tax and national insurance, disregarded by the psychiatrist because it was the past. However, what I did in voluntary terms at this later stage had importance because I was contributing to society. It didn't mean that I wouldn't soon return to full-time paid employment that fitted the employability and life skills I had.

I like to reflect on those five years as my time out. Having the freedom to be me and getting part of my family back was rewarding.

To give one example of what I did then, I helped set up my dad's family business in Essex. My role in this could have easily become a full-time one in the future. Given my difficult pecuniary circumstances it was too expensive for me to commute between Essex and Norfolk on a regular basis. Once it was running I acted as an adviser from a distance.

Back in March 2001, when we began writing this book, I remember how deep my frustration and anger had become. "I want the operation now," I raged, the unrecognisable sound blaring through my wall suiting my juvenile neighbour's perverse taste in music and almost driving me to violence.

"They're conditioned to show no compassion," I ranted, "trained from a book that shows them there's only one way to treat us poor, pathetic, deluded souls appearing before them and that's according to Randell's law."[1] I felt the doctors and psychiatrists were working against me.

A few of the things they said hurt. I got irritated over this power trip business. Unfortunately, I had to bend their way. To be me I needed the powerful whether I got on with them or not. We had repeatedly covered the same ground. Wasn't that damaging enough? It ate away at my self-esteem. How could I believe in myself when the vibe I kept getting from them was I didn't look and behave like a genuine woman? I felt powerless. At one appointment I was told: "If you want me to do this for you get here punctually."

Doctors can be late, patients can't, no matter what the reason. This one didn't care I'd had to travel a hundred and eighty miles. He probably only lived a short walk from the hospital. I had been up for hours and was tired. The traffic was against me all the way as it was the morning rush hour. Also during the same consultation, he said: "Why didn't you come down last night and stay in a hotel?"

"You think I'm rich?" I struck back at him. My lack of money was a fact I had brought to his attention frequently that in itself was enough to bring me to breaking point. He dismissed this. Instead, he told me to "Get a job". I couldn't win. What was right for me wasn't hunky-dory. He insisted: "If you want my help you do what I say."

Perhaps inevitably, given the seriousness of gender realignment surgery with its uncertain psychological and physical outcome, I had spent years waiting for my operation. "When?" I asked constantly.

"When you're ready," replied one psychiatrist, that to me meant: "When you conform" or rather "Until you submit to our way of doing this."

Determined to succeed, I refused to give up any of the headway I had made during my exhausting campaign. I wasn't there to kowtow to them: I was there to be me.

By then I had convinced myself that no amount of so-called professional assistance and guidance would alter my course. Counselling was neither here nor there: I wanted to manage my own life. Why did I have to attend quarterly appointments for that? It was the same at Charing Cross. Four visits a year. They told me: "We explore all the pros and cons with you because if we don't there is the possibility you might regret having the surgery further down the line."

What exactly were the things I said and did that caused them to worry? I was more likely to lose it due to the goading tenor of their continual questioning. I wanted to take responsibility for what was essential to my successful development. It was my choice. I was mature and stable enough to make it and deal with the consequences.

Note

1 Randell's Law is according to psychiatrist John Randell who challenged the beliefs of those suffering from gender dysphoria to ensure they were serious about their desire for gender realignment.

Chapter Twenty-one

In March 2001 I had neighbour problems. Arriving at my flat one humid Thursday morning with David to discuss a plan for writing this book I heard the bass pumping out of the sound system in the property next door. "Drugs 'r' us are in," I snapped, raising my voice as I slammed all of my living room windows shut. I looked out on to the road below, the only sense of real space I could grab in those moments of frustration.

The lad who was causing the disturbance had his mates with him. Thumping bass blocked out any tune there might have been lying beneath it, struggling to break through. Settling down, David and I began to talk. Throughout our conversation, originally recorded on an ailing Dictaphone, the loud pulsing niggled at us, mimicking some form of Second World War Japanese psychological torture, pummelling our thoughts, similar to unwanted interference from a foreign wireless broadcast cutting into our chosen programme and ruining it. The commotion was worse at night, permeating the walls of my flat and all parts of me, an invisible hammer tapping my nerves. I was a bomb waiting to go off.

In the early hours, the tubercular looking Harry Spring living below had what sounded like an air compressor running, with the raucous effect of a generator powering a pneumatic drill at a road works. We were exposed to the strains of the sixties, not unpleasant under normal circumstances, but when the voices of Shirley Bassey and Dusty Springfield were repeated constantly from Spring's knackered old speakers, it did my head in; reminiscent of a badly received pirate radio station coming up through the floor, there was no escaping discord in that flat. At certain intervals, the din had the effect of either living next door to an aircraft hangar containing a Lancaster bomber with all its engines running, or the London underground.

Once I moved from the hostel at Cromer to my flat in North Walsham I thought I had left behind the virtually nonstop racket

I used to tolerate. How wrong I was. Just as I had started to settle the nightmare began. I had to tough out worse noise levels than I put up with from all the boys and girls at the Saint Matthew Housing accommodation where periodically there were eight records playing at once.

I lived over the top of Mister Inconsiderate himself, my freedom to be relatively comfortable there restricted by his behaviour. Apparently, because he could spread a bit of margarine on a slice of bread and find his mouth to put it in, Harold Spring was free to impose his selfish lifestyle on me. I believed he was a health risk. Whoever made the decision to move him to our patch didn't think about the poor, afflicted mortals he would live near and the effect he could have on them. Their priority was keeping this person and others like him out of institutionalised care.

Totally dysfunctional, the master of designer antisocial behaviour's cacophony ensured I was never able to go to bed when I wanted. It didn't end there. That row reminding me of an air compressor replaced the one from his sound system with a vibration of a different kind, running on and off all night. Amazed that he could open and shut a door on fifty occasions in an hour, I realised I would struggle to cope with these disturbances.

At twelve-thirty one morning, through my persistent badgering of the council environmental health department, one of its representatives sat in my bedroom, told me he wouldn't be able to live in my den, then left. He never came back.

Can you believe one of the usual suspects was allowed to poison our lawns? Two years went by with the grass still dead until, following several complaints, it was treated. We all paid a service charge for the gardens and green areas linked to the properties to be kept nice. These were supposed to be capable citizens who could live responsibly in the neighbourhood the state had let loose on us. Being a person who really likes to see those who have been unable to handle life get better and rejoin society I am not insulting folk who do this and show at least vague signs of an ability to mix with their neighbours to form a pleasant community. What laws there are to protect citizens with a social conscience appear to me to be so hard to enforce no one bothers to make the effort to use them when they are necessary. They had nowhere else to put Spring. I had to like it, lump it, or move, and you guessed it - I wasn't moving.

By 8th June 2001 there was still no definite news about my operation. For the last three years I had been informed that I was near the top of the waiting list. I told several of my friends then looked as if I had been lying to them because another year ended and I still hadn't got my date.

I went through a lonely phase when I desperately sought company. Although I had been able to cope with being by myself for a while, the isolation got to me. An increasing awareness of social problems made me concerned for the welfare of my friends and their children. My approach to life became one of wanting to help others, and particularly my fellow sufferers.

When I blame the world for my predicament, that is me working out my frustration. These outbursts are releases of tension that build up inside me then come out when there is no room for any more. In the spring of 2001 I was fifty years old and stagnating. I became more conscious of my biological clock ticking away: I was afraid of not having much time left as me.

The pettiness of my neighbour sparked a ludicrous row that made what was important a thousandfold harder to ride out. Cornered by Spring because my cat was allegedly interfering with his, we had a run in by my car that was parked near the entrance to our flats. While our cats were probably playing together on the lawn out the back, chasing each other as they often did being male and female, we were locked in dispute.

Pointing his bony finger at my face, my neighbour had asked for more than a bit of trouble from me. That he could stand there arguing about a cat telling me he had his first and I shouldn't have one spelled out to me the depressing fact that I had come to the one part of this estate where evolution had stopped.

For a few seconds I lost it and pushed him up against my car. I got my temper back under control, my mind saying: "Don't hit him. Remember what happened outside Cromer Jobcentre."

Bounding towards us was a male I put in the same category as Spring, shouting: "Let him go." On arriving at the fracas, panting out his words that I couldn't quite hear at first, he thrust his contorted face into mine, sucking in my space as he breathed.

"If you don't leave him alone I'll punch your balls where you won't find them," said the man. Staring out this bloke as he got threateningly close, I put him straight.

"Hormone therapy shrank them so you'd be wasting your time," I reacted, thinking honesty was the best policy. His silence was satisfying.

This piece of street theatre drew an audience who all came to my defence; I didn't need it.

I'm going to have you done in," he continued. "It's already been arranged."

Like a little Jack Russell snapping at Spring and his bodyguard's feet, one of my helpful neighbours, Katie, failed to listen to my advice to stay back and leave me to settle this alone. She began shouting at the pair. Thoroughly bored with the situation, I returned to my flat. My cat was curled up in my chair, purring away happily. I eavesdropped on Katie ranting outside my window until she and the sad ones went home out of boredom as well.

All this leads me to wonder whether I am the right person to give advice and guidance to others now I am cured. Here I am going on about how everyone should understand me. What if I had to help the likes of Harold Spring?

David remembered a situation in which he found himself in 1999 where one of society's marginalised could easily have been judged at face value when there was actually a deeper, positive side to this person's character. It was during the period he was working for Norfolk Voluntary Services on their Mental Health Befriending

Scheme that David had a client called Reg who was in his fifties. Reg had suffered more than one nervous breakdown in his life. Living in a flat he enjoyed a degree of independence on a social security benefit with the support of a Community Psychiatric Nurse, social worker and housing association adviser. The moment David first saw Reg on his own he appeared very agitated. During later visits, at odd intervals Reg would get up to pace the room and look out of the window that had a prime view down on to the road below and the path leading from it that formed the approach to his block.[1]

When Reg talked about his mum and dad there was warmth in his eyes. He said: "I didn't have this hassle when they were alive," illustrating how our emotional attachments give us meaning and reason for being. David is close to his parents and could identify with Reg from this point of view, putting aside any diagnostic or other label to focus on his uniqueness.[2]

What David wanted from this project was to experience my way of being without thinking of me as transsexual.[3] A basic norm of human society is to conform to a bi-polarised gender system.[4] That I had been diagnosed as 'gender dysphoric' or, in layman's terms, 'transsexual', meant I was unhappy with my biological male classification. I wanted to be accepted wholly as my psychological gender, which is female. The alternative of me being considered genderless in a gendered society would have been unworkable.[5]

I shared with David entries from my journal, written about 1997, when I was living at the hostel. In this extract, I talk about how my true gender forms the basis of my whole identity. Moreover, while I had been given the diagnostic label, 'gender dysphoric', my expression of this indisposition could be seen simply as a unique way of being.

"Those of us who have suffered from gender dysphoria know that during our worst episodes we thought and felt in similarly dramatic ways. I realise that led me to behave badly. Unable to offer insight into the individual differences between us,

I can at least share my biography with others in the hope it will help them.

We knew what we had to do and often took different paths to achieve it. When we shared an identical route we didn't all get off at the same stop; a few of us went on longer journeys."

If an interviewer asked people who are or in my case were gender dysphoric what it is like, they could most probably generalise about it although they wouldn't be able to describe the phenomenon right down to the subtlest details of their emotions and cognitions, all of which are difficult to capture in words.[6][7] You have to feel a person's feelings and think their thoughts the way they feel and think them for you to understand the exact nature of them. It would be wonderful if everyone could appreciate and empathise with me as the person I really am and I was able to respond in kind.

You can see how much I cared what the masses thought of me when I wrote that around 1997.

Another piece from my journal of the late 1990s shows how frustrated I was by then.

"The course of action I continue to take is the right one for me even if I have to struggle at every moment along the way to reach my goal. I have left it late, but I couldn't have dealt with it until I was ready. Now it is urgent I get it done before I am too old. I am sick of pretending to be someone else."

That is how I saw it. Standing in a room, surrounded by my friends, I would have behaved as I believed they wanted me to rather than be me.

Typically, I would do this to avoid the risk of losing them, which, in hindsight, was a sad way to think. It is clear to me now that whatever happened only my true friends would stand by me. The ones who wanted me to look and behave in ways acceptable to them would have rejected me if I hadn't. Some abuse their friendships with others by using them for their own ends. Only the folk I can trust are my genuine allies. Those who wanted me to conform rigorously to their expectations soon went out of my life. It wasn't just extremely judgmental acquaintances and colleagues who demanded this. For me, society was saying: "If you look male how can you be female? Be male or else." Where does the "Be male or else" come from? I think of all the years I was subject to masculine role conditioning from early childhood onwards, and not wanting any part of that. Imagine a small bunch of opponents holding you down, your thrashing about having no effect; that is how it feels. Barely able to breathe, almost no room to move, I built up a ferocious energy that gave me the strength to break free. I hope readers will consider that however negatively they perceive inoffensive, non-threatening, but relatively unusual looking fellow citizens at first glance, it is constructive and progressive to treat them with kindness.

What about these unusual individual differences? When are they not acceptable? How does society make that clear? What is being done to improve public knowledge of how to respond appropriately to the discredited or stigmatised?

I suggest gender dysphoria is an issue that is more avoided than faced up to. In my opinion, discussing it is still socially and politically incorrect. The bigoted will not abide individuals who in their view have crossed a forbidden line to be themselves.

How do I judge a person when I first see them? We form our own ideas about one another that we use to explain what we are like.

Say I meet a man. He appears to me in a certain way. I make assumptions about him based on my past experiences, information I have gathered through my senses and accounts from a variety of sources.

I judge him by the way he looks at me, his body language, what he says to me and how he says it. The surroundings and the vibe of the place I meet him in also affect the way I see him.

This is what American Gestalt psychologist Solomon Asch called implicit personality theory. We ourselves are psychologists summing up the individual traits and qualities of others as a whole. Implicit personality theory is a term used to describe our unconscious methods of working things out that allow us to form impressions of people on very little information. To me, this person I have just bumped into looks shy and withdrawn, therefore I have expectations of him being so.

If I met a man whom I knew had a reputation for violence and on first acquaintance sensed there might be some truth in this, I would deal with him carefully. Whether extrovert or introvert, my perception of him would be organised around my idea of the potential harm he could cause me. Another may read him as simply either sociable or reserved without noticing anything unusual or threatening. What individuals look like, the verbal and non-verbal signs they show, and what we believe about them already, assist us in deciding if they are a danger to us. Our implicit personality theories can help us live together safely and productively.

Fritz Heider, an Austrian psychologist, developed an account of social perception called attribution theory. The following is only my interpretation of a set of principles showing how we explain the causes of certain behaviours and events. An attribution is a quality or characteristic we attach to ourselves, other people, or objects, that suggests a reason or reasons why something has happened. I attributed to myself feminine qualities and traits that, taken as a whole, gave me the strong belief that I was a woman in spite of my biological male body. Due to this, for most of my life I have worked at developing my feminine appearance and way of being, which has led me to perform desired behaviours that fit our culture's criteria for living as a woman.

A diverse range of roles in society have specific features that define them and also contribute to our explanations of certain causes and effects. Social roles are the parts we play when belonging to groups. With every one we take on our behaviour has to meet the requirements attached to it, which are decided by what society needs it to achieve in a safe and healthy way.

We each of us play out many roles in a single day, like friend, partner, father, mother, pupil, mentor, and employee. Social norms are unwritten rules giving us a strong notion of what sort of behaviour or way of life is expected of us when we belong to a particular group or organisation.

Traditional ideas of what it is to be male and female are too simplistic. Certainly they do not capture how I truly feel, behave, or how I define myself as a woman. Men have traits previously thought of as exclusively feminine, and women those that were at one time considered attributable to men only.

We can think of all members of a group as conforming to a pattern or way of being that never changes such as the idea that politicians always use words skilfully to obscure unpalatable truths about their beliefs and actions. Here we are building stereo-types and this example is a negative and ludicrous generalisation of what politicians are like. Think of those who work hard for their constituents and try to make the world a fairer and healthier place. Occasionally stereotypes can be useful in that they help us form a general picture of the way specific groups - rather than individuals that is covered by the implicit personality theory - act, and what their purpose is. For example, conscientious advisers, mentors and counsellors are trustworthy and concerned for our welfare because they adhere diligently to strict ethical standards and their main objective is to guide clients towards a level of self-awareness that can facilitate a better quality of life. As we have seen though, stereotypes can be superficial. I look beneath the surface, uncovering the truth about my contacts, refusing to accept what I think initially or have been told they are like. Of course, I am no Saint. I often get it wrong. When I talk about kindness to others I do mean those who don't interfere with my or anyone else's well-being, hence my problem with Spring when he lived in the flat beneath me.

A typical attitude towards gender dysphorics is that they are all sexual perverts. Prejudiced observers actually start believing this is true.

In human psychology, there are three components to attitudes: knowledge, feeling, and behavioural. Those who find difficulty in understanding gender dysphoria may fear it. That can be reinforced by further negative information: their dislike of members of society who have the disparity could be made worse by watching a biased media portrayal of sufferers, strengthening the false belief that every gender dysphoric person is weird.

The behavioural elements of such an attitude, that follows from a general loathing of transsexuals, might be avoidance, verbal abuse, or physical violence. If the critics' knowledge aspect is weak, the picture they get will be distorted. It must be strong for them to distinguish what is real. I may not like some folk when I first meet them; I hope I would get all the relevant facts before I made up my mind about their character. Discrimination against individuals or groups can be direct or indirect affecting all aspects of life such as issues relating to sex, race, religion and body shape. For ages I have worried about how people might react to me. Suffice to say that prejudice exists in the human condition as a quality that can be made less severe by improved knowledge leading to greater tolerance of individual differences. Realistically, as far as we know, intolerance, like a violent tendency, may never be completely removed from human thinking no matter what educational policies and laws are passed and implemented to protect the vulnerable, unless advances in genetic engineering can, in a sense, eliminate the biological part of what causes it.

Notes

1 *Reg looked uncomfortable. The faintest sound of a car approaching would cause him to stand up and walk briskly over to a window. He could not keep still at first, then as I began to chat to him he settled gradually.*

2 *When I first met Carol I knew her diagnosis, yet I was determined not to treat her as if she was mentally ill. I found myself before an individual rather than a patient with a diagnostic label, gender dysphoria, slapped on her by medical professionals, by which she had been defined. Over time, I came to appreciate her ability to cross the restrictive boundaries of gender dysphoria to show me her true self.*

3 *If we adjust our perspective to actively listen to someone who has a difference that can be stigmatised, such as a gender identity disorder or mental illness, we may empathise with them, and instead of experiencing an individual with a discrediting label attached, discover a unique human being.*

4 *This is classifying the sex of individuals as either male or female. Some people choose not to conform to this and they are apparently gender neutral or without gender.*

5 *A life without gender in a gendered society is difficult for most of us to imagine, let alone practise. Intersex is a way of being where a person is born neither completely male nor female. Virtually one in fifty enter this world with an irregularity of sexual development. Even so, as we have studied, our society finds it hard to understand and give appropriate support to these. Say a person whose gender at birth was classified as female and as an adult dresses in black, shaves their head, actively avoids behaviours that we usually associate with femininity and refuses to be called either male or female. What are the implications of this? Although it could be assumed that their attitude and behaviour are more likely to be based on misguided fantasy than something that is real, we do not know what an individual who perceives themselves to be gender neutral feels and thinks down to the finest detail, therefore, I argue, we cannot judge them. Perhaps it can be accepted that a non-gendered way of being exists and those who feel they are non-gendered should also have the protection of equality laws.*

6 *Carol is aware of herself seeing, hearing, touching, tasting, and smelling things in the world around her. Her what are known as qualia are the specific nature or qualities of these sense impressions she has: her thoughts, including memories, and feelings, in vivid detail, subtly different in character from those of other people, say, when in love,*

tasting food, driving a car, visiting a favourite seaside resort, and so on. All these are apprehended in forms unique to her. Her physical appearance has been adjusted to match her ways of feeling and thinking like a woman.

7 *"Sense and Sensibility", Lodge, David. The Guardian, 2 November 2002.*

Chapter Twenty-two

When I was confused I found keeping my diary helped. That gave me a way of putting all my feelings and thoughts in order. Poems were included in this, a selection of which follow.

With whom I identify

I look at you and I see me,
The me who I would like to be,
You radiate life with girlish charm,
I know that this can do you no harm.
The strength you have from deep within,
Will pull you through and you will win,
You hate me now for what I do,
But the me you see wants to be like you.

From anger to love

My anger, released through the pen,
Helping me calm the turmoil within,
I have so much to say and do,
Maybe that will get me through,
Although the words come out in a mess,
I hope from these you'll be able to guess,
What I say is from my heart,
I'll do my best before we part.

This dual life I lead

I hope the day will come
When I can shout I am just one;
Will I ever be freed
From this dual life I lead?

Can they be who they really are?

As I walk along a busy street,
What of the people I'm bound to meet?
Are they held back by all the hype?
Are they like me feeling life's not right?

Can they cope with the truth so far?
Can they express who they really are?
Or are their lives a total mess
Through needs they're trying hard to suppress?

I'll be all right

I have come through the mist into ninety-six,
But identity problems still persist,
I'll use this year to sort my priority,
In ninety-seven escape authority,
Following the appointment changing my life,
That will start to make everything all right.

C is for courage to do what must be done.
A is for anger that festers within me.
R is for remembering any good times there might have been.
O is for only being myself from now on.
L is for love for the kind people I know.

R is for remorse for all I have done wrong.
O is for operation that will change my life.
Y is for yesterdays with all their hurt.
C is for completion which is what I strive for.
E is for euphoria when I am essentially female.

Diane wrote this poem for me which I wanted to include here.

Quite A 'Gal' Is Carol

I gazed at her long russet locks,
And delicious blue-grey eyes,
Her figure long and slender,
With split skirt up to her thighs,
She's very kind and caring,
As honest as the day,
She's witty and intelligent,
And will always have her say.

Carol's waiting for the postman,
To bring a letter for her 'Op',
Which will make her a true woman,
For as part man she is not.

I am always glad to see her,
When she calls in time for tea,
And have social services to thank,
For introducing her to me.

Diane Berthelot

This was what I wrote when I knew the surgery was likely to go ahead:

"12th May 2001: I have heard from Doctor Olive and Barbara Ross that I've got an appointment to discuss my operation at last. I am walking around as if I have been accepted. I'm scared to pick up the phone to ask one of them outright. I hope it's my turn."

Of course, although later than expected, I had the procedure and it was a success. Everyone who knew me and understood was happy for me. My close friend Gail was particularly supportive.

One Spring Bank Holiday weekend I went to a barbecue with a trusted companion. The celebrations went well until a clueless know-all referred to me as 'him'. Nearly every opportunity I took to find a progressive social milieu an acquaintance aware of my history had to tactlessly inform others that I used to be male and was currently - if you pardon the irony of what invariably turned out to be an absurd and utterly ridiculous semantic game - in a sort of no man's or woman's land. "Is it something I'm doing wrong?" I kept asking myself. Once I am seen as male by any individual this impression is locked in their brain and I have a terrible job trying to convince them otherwise. If anyone was to ask me discreetly I wouldn't have a problem telling them. It is when a person decides they need to do the job for me and without thinking uses the wrong words that upsets me. They say: "By the way, Carol used to be a man." Should I resolve to explain myself, I tell those concerned I was gender dysphoric. There is a whole different, appropriate way of describing it for those who want to listen.

If a man showed interest in me I would tell him about my background and circumstances, pointing out that after surgery, as one might expect, eventually a proportion of male-to-female gender dysphorics have intimate relationships with men: in the wider society this tends to be considered homosexual because of failure to acknowledge they are female and unable to function sexually as a male. Where a female partner is chosen - which could be due to having difficulty relating to males, haunted by memories of pretending to be one - they are used to living as resourceful, independent women enjoying close, high disclosure friendships with girlfriends. I have spoken to many male-to-female gender dysphorics going through the real life test and they told me they don't want to be with men because it reminds them of their old life. The what might be perceived by some as generally aggressive approach of males is what the post-operative male-to-female gender dysphoric wants to get away from.

I have learned that once I tell anybody who I am they do one of two things. They either go away to think about the situation they have found themselves in then reappear at a later date or they walk off and never come back. If they do return then we have reached the next stage, giving me hope that the friendship will survive.

Considering British society today is freed up enough to allow the masses to express their diverse sexual identities, it is frustrating to find that I am still being treated as if I am playing my former male role. At that barbecue judgement was passed on me. It strikes me that although honesty is a good policy by the way it clears the air letting people know where they stand, it can also cause hell.

I had to reveal the truth about my new life. The longer I put that off the more I hurt my loved ones. Lies built up until a mountain of untruths led to dreadful consequences when social pressures finally challenged them. My emotional life exploded. Being sincere and up front without delay is a wise move that will hopefully limit the damage. The result is the difference between a firework going off and, if the issue remains hidden for a long span as in my circumstances, an atom bomb with fallout. Whichever way I look at it now those who were important in my life had to be told as soon as possible. It would never have been easy to take.

I once asked Andy of Saint Matthew Housing in Cromer whether he thought I was sexy. His answer was: "Yes, you're sexy - in a masculine sort of way." This shocked me. I had spent a year trying not to be masculine. Thinking he fancied me and knowing I was definitely attracted to him, his declaration took the kick out of the wine I drank. Its flavour was suddenly more a cheap mouth wash than the appealing taste I was savouring only moments before. Was he comparing me with his old girlfriends? I didn't have muscles, I was slim, and I dressed nice. He later told me he couldn't get across what he wanted to say. His words came out wrong. Maybe that is why I am always seeking reassurance from whoever will give it to me.

The male-to-female gender dysphoric is inclined to be large and the female-to-male small. Males are prone to having big feet. Thinning hair on the head, killed off by testosterone - another disadvantage for the male-to-female - can be first endured in their teens. Scientists have come up with a medication that can restore hair growth as long as the root hasn't perished. Apparently, even when you have lost hair the actual root can take up to twenty years to die. This medication has to be given under a doctor's supervision. At this stage of writing, the percentage of those who could be helped was as high as eighty-five.

I did not believe what I have described above applied to me. It really hurt to think that when Andy looked at me he saw a man in drag.

His comment led me to want to justify my way of being because I was worried about his perception of me. A woman can add a little masculinity to her feminine dress code and still be accepted as female: she is no less one for putting on a few clothes generally thought of as those more commonly worn by males. Through wearing trousers she may not feel so vulnerable in a male dominated work environment.

I only have to walk around the city a short while to spot a number of women who look what I call assertive or even power dressed for reasons that might include discouraging unwanted male attention; it is probably because it makes them comfortable. A male observing a female dressed in a suit generally would not, I hope, think she is a woman wanting to be a man: I would like to believe he could entertain the idea of her as one who has decided to express her femininity in an assertive way. Women dress up for the day and watch what happens. When this alters the power balance of their relationships with men the sense of being in control can be exhilarating. The main aim for me, however, and I bet this is the case for most women, is not playing games to achieve gender one-upmanship (excuse the pun) or out of rivalry; rather, to feel at ease in my own skin, confident and happy.

For the sake of illustration, I want to use a stereotype I will call the macho type of male. Macho walks around in his own beloved space he has created for himself. That is his battleground. If it is invaded by other males, Macho is inclined to defend it. Certain men have no problem walking straight up to a woman and entering her body buffer zone, the outcome of which depends on how much she wants him there. Nature is telling this guy: "Look, there's a female. Your genes can be passed on." If Macho invades the turf of a rival and won't leave there may be a head-to-head that in our hunter-gatherer days might have meant a fight to the death. I can imagine you saying to yourselves: "If it is so brilliant in the male-dominated world why would you want to leave it?" The answer is: if I had been able to tolerate my male body I could have walked around less taut; I still would have felt out of kilter. If you are convinced you are not male it is obviously pointless trying to be one whatever social advantages that is supposed to give you, yet no one can deny I once functioned this way and that related characteristics surfaced in me which had both drawbacks and benefits. On the down side, for example, I could drive like a maniac, be excessively confrontational, violent; on the up, decisive and risk-taking. These might be recognised as behaviours those of the masculine sex show more readily.

By contrast, nowadays, focusing on the practical details of enhancing my femininity, make-up can be a problem. Arguably more important than getting my clothes right, if I think I look decent in the mirror in that what I am wearing makes my skin appear naturally feminine, this has a desirable effect on the way I behave, which in turn influences how positively others view me. Appearance and deportment need constant attention to become second nature. A male-to-female gender dysphoric only has what she has picked up during brief moments of trying to be herself that in my case were interrupted by large chunks of male role socialisation forced on me.

If I had told Andy all this perhaps he could have recognised me as I wished? That would not have been enough for me though: I wanted him to regard me as an attractive woman.

I hope whoever reads this will get closer to understanding what it is like to be gender dysphoric through accounts of my adventures. On a wider scale, ideally my story shows the value of welcoming and supporting those whose complex and challenging differences from others are still part of the rich diversity of human existence from which much can be learned and enjoyed.

Am I cured? I am the same person, developing in the right direction.

I can now start using my energy to live rather than struggle. The process goes on. When do I actually become everything I am capable of becoming? I believe we are never complete. There is always potential for further evolvement and no limit to what can be. It hasn't suddenly become easy - end of story – and that's it. I wish. In the ebb and flow of a human life, one day it looks like progress is being made, the next there is nothing but hopelessness and despair. Both are part of what it is to be human.

Presently, I am growing and developing behind the scenes. My period of adjustment and reflection is coming to an end. I am ready to live.

Chapter Twenty-three

Learning from the views and anecdotes of others has helped me become more open-minded about life's possibilities. Through interviewing Damon, plus two confidantes, I thought I would get a useful picture of how gender and sexuality enriched their sense of personal identity.

While at school, Damon saw himself as a heterosexual young man who did everything he imagined would be expected of a teenage male with the commonplace preference for the opposite sex. He didn't remember having any gay feelings up to the age of sixteen. What he did say was that when he reached puberty he started straying from his old path, explaining this by using the term 'gradual metamorphosis' because it was the beginning of a slow process that transformed his sexuality. I asked Damon: "Are you gay?" "No," he insisted. "I regard myself as an intellectual bisexual. I like the idea of bisexuality. It's all in my head: in other words, I'm a virtual bisexual rather than a practising one. The freedom I have to imagine myself in and play the bisexual male role without labelling myself or being labelled as belonging to any one particular sexual orientation is exciting."

Totally at ease with girls, Damon had no problem being in female company. In fact, he loved it.

"Generally speaking, they seem relaxed about discussing issues down under." He wasn't talking about Australia here, by the way. "Buying knickers, for instance, is natural to them, yet I bet there are a lot of blokes who aren't comfortable purchasing underwear for themselves. Girls are also able to hold three conversations at once without losing track of the themes and issues they are about. They're more in the moment with gay men because there's no sexual pressure and that type of male's feminised world is compatible with theirs because it's similar."

Adding that he felt protected when around females, Damon celebrated his freedom to talk openly about girlie concerns and passions when in their presence. He became part of the sisterhood: it was as if his identity merged with theirs to form an emotionally supportive whole.

"I don't consider myself relationship material," he confessed, "but when I do meet someone who I believe is right for me it often turns out to be me falling for them. Sex is less important than the greater picture of simply being myself. I am what I am and there's no changing that."

Although he admitted his way of being had caused him problems, from his point of view these were largely down to others' attitudes towards him. It was their ignorance of who he really was that caused them to misconstrue his lifestyle, he told me. He was adamant that his sexuality was so personalised that he found it difficult to pin it down for anybody unable to grasp things that were not black and white. He also felt as I do that one's sex life is such a private, unique affair, he would only want to share details of his with close friends like me who could embrace as well as appreciate what it is like for him.

Damon occasionally aims to shock. He manages to get in and out of bizarre situations as this following section of conversation between us suggests, opening with his favoured view of himself:

"I am a chameleon. I like to imagine I can change from one state to another depending on whose company I'm in. If I'm with straight guys I can blend with them. It's more like putting on a show. I can also switch the other way round and in a group of gay males having a laugh be more camp: really limp-wristed and shocking."

"You're a person who fits eroticism into your life in varied and transient ways?"

"If people want to assume I'm gay, let them, if they think of me as bisexual, so what? I'm me and that's all that matters."

"What if you really fancied someone who disapproved of your more outrageous behaviour?"

"I'd finish with them," he replied, "and these are the reasons why:

1) If they couldn't accept me as I am they wouldn't fit in with many of my friends. To me love is being compatible in every area of the connection which has to be worked at all the time. It's about having to adapt to another person. This leopard doesn't change his spots to order and a potential desire for me to do this is no foundation on which to build a happy, lasting relationship.

2) I believe in being honest and insist that my sexuality - which as far as I'm concerned has no label but is best described as ambivalent - doesn't need paraphrasing to anyone. I usually keep a comfortable distance between myself and those who are interested in me sexually. I'd be more at ease in a romantic and sexual partnership that's formed and developed in a non-judgmental atmosphere with no strings attached because any there would get pulled. I'd feel choked leading me to think my partner was taking over. There has to be equality."

Here was someone who had control over how he felt and who he got involved with. "Who's he kidding?" I asked myself.

I interviewed a further two of my friends. The first was a young, open-minded girl full of the emotions you would expect passing through the early stages of womanhood. She is following a straight line with her sexuality, how she perceives herself, and where she belongs. It is apparently the usual step-by-step pattern of human growth and development that she is experiencing: young girl grows into a woman, has boyfriends, and eventually a husband or partner, forming a stable relationship, with children. She had no sexual identity or preference issues while she was young, as she put it.

"Nature got it right for me," she said.

"That was a little dig at me, I think," I told her. She laughed.

"Although I feel like this today that's not to say I will tomorrow. I've no thoughts about same sex coupling or wanting to be a different gender to what I am."

"There you go again," I said.

"Now you're acting paranoid," she responded. "I love being female and what goes with it even though it has its downside. My periods can be difficult to put up with. No. Bloody painful is what I meant to say."

She said that as if menstruation really is the curse of womanhood. Liz believed men should go through a bodily cycle like this then maybe they would understand. It made me think that at the height of the pain and inconvenience of the monthly drag a lot of women would share her view. In defence of men, most have to shave - those who don't grow beards, that is - and depending on the sensitivity of their skin, that can be uncomfortable. We agreed it still wasn't as much suffering as what women had to put up with. Shaving was more a minor inconvenience.

If males had to have babies there would only be one child per family. While this may solve the problem of overcrowding on the planet it would also bring the human race to an end. That is why God didn't leave the tough side of reproduction to males.

Liz traced her life from entering puberty to our interview. I was surprised she had trouble talking about herself. She was shy at first and wanted prompting, finding it easier to respond to my questions than struggle to remember her story in chronological order. This is a summary of Liz's views:

I went to a girls' school. My only contact with boys was on the bus journey there and back. I was fifteen before I took any active interest in them. This lad asked me out. There was no bond. We never got past the kissing stage. I was seventeen when I had my first real boyfriend. He was all I knew about love and sex. I had nothing to compare him with.

It wasn't how I thought it was going to be. I was locked in that affair for three and a half years; it stopped me from growing as a person. I'd always gone to the corner shop out of habit because it felt safe when really that was leading to an insecure future and the alternative - if I'd had the courage to explore it - would have brought me new, albeit unsettling character building challenges, preparing me for greater opportunities. Finding the giant superstore of life gave me choice and the freedom to choose.

My former partner had to control my day right down to who I talked to on the phone. He was booking my life in advance. At one point he arranged for us to go to Burton on Trent to visit my relatives. Sex was him on top and no love. I told him: "No." He still went thrusting on. I'd cry half way through. I didn't and still don't call it rape. It was consensual in the weakest sense of that word. I was hoping he'd show some spark of emotion.

I've gone into a new relationship. My current partner helped me escape the first when he was just a friend and we ended up getting involved. We've got too much for each other now and we're cooling off. I like to look on it as a bit of space for us to work out what we both want.

He says: "We'll be mates. I'll see you later."

He's thirty, a bachelor, and wants to date me when it's convenient to him: he fits me into his schedule. That's not good enough for me.

The other day I enjoyed a girlie night out with my friend, Jess. I wanted to prove to myself I was still attractive, and I did. There was a guy in the pub who showed a fleeting interest in me. His hair was like my boyfriend's and I started to go wobbly. I would never have taken it any further.

I'm comfortable in male company and I enjoy sex with my boyfriend. I aim to be his partner, not his part-time escort: I want to commit myself to our partnership and him to act the mature, responsible man he should be at thirty."

Liz was convinced that owning the label 'girlfriend' made at least one of her roles clear giving her life purpose and meaning which led to a more stable sense of self.

Helen was approaching forty when I interviewed her, and had been married with two children both of whom had grown up and left home. She had a job and a car. When she was young she liked being a girl, not that the differences between the sexes bothered her. She remarked that while she was a teenager her life was fantastic:

"We spent our time talking about boys, clothes, and who we'd marry. Really we were fantasising. As a teenage girl I wasn't promiscuous. I never dated anybody until I was seventeen. My first boyfriend was a year older than me and that made me feel great, plus the fact he was good looking - or was to me. He must have been to others as well because a lot of girls wanted to date him. I fell in love. It was a year before we slept together, not that he didn't try to persuade me to a lot earlier in our relationship. Today youngsters prioritise sex. They live more for the moment than the future and, it appears, think if sex with their partner is all right they might as well cohabit. Both my children are separated from their partners and they're in their early twenties. It's sad that lives are damaged because the sexual behaviour of many is reckless. One-parent families appear to be the norm.

I met my husband when we were both eighteen. After a short engagement we tied the knot. It was hard at first but however difficult things could be we were in love. I relied on my mum for advice and support. I was an only child and although people say we are spoilt I think we also miss out by not having siblings to refer to and compare ourselves with. When I was first married I used to ask mum all sorts of questions. I wanted children and as it happened I had a boy and a girl close together. There is only a year between them. Sadly, my husband died in a car crash five years ago. My daughter has become my friend like I did with my mum.

She pops round most days to make sure I'm okay, and sometimes we go shopping together."

"Don't you miss male company?" I asked Helen. She responded with bold, fleeting amusement showing through a playful smile on her face and a brief air of relish in the tone of her voice.

"You mean, do I miss sex? Yes. My husband and I enjoyed a healthy sex life. We had our ups and downs though we always put matters right with a cuddle and this often ended in us making love. That's how we dealt with any upsets. I don't want to see anybody else romantically, or at least not yet. I have platonic male friends at work and go out with them. That's it. I am a woman and proud to be one both emotionally and sexually.

I notice things going on around me I don't like. Generally I feel sorry for the men and women who do them."

"What are these things you don't like?" I probed.

"I've nothing against gay people in general. I'd like to think I have an open mind when it comes to talking about human sexuality. There's a difference between same sex partners on their own and those bringing up children though."

For Helen, the whole idea of a gay couple being parents was a deviation from the norm.

"I think children should have both a mum and a dad. They need that balance of a male and female role model while they're growing up, and to get used to the idea of the difference between males and females so they know how to behave appropriately in their roles as sons or daughters.

There was a news item on television about the rights of two gay men to be parents. Had they given any thought to what long term effects their actions could have on their adopted children? I'd say the same thing if two gay women said they wanted to bring up a child."

I decided to end our chat there. Helen held the view that children adopted by same sex parents are more likely to be confused by having two male or two female ones, which could make them emotionally unstable and possibly lead to distorted sex role socialisation causing gender and identity problems later in life. Once they get to school age awkward questions like: "Why have you got two daddies (or two mummies?)" might be early warning signs that a child is a likely target for bullying.

Her opinion is of course speculative. We don't know what the outcome of particular same sex partners raising children will be. Frankly, why shouldn't we trust them to be capable of providing youngsters with a loving family home and bringing them up to be balanced adults, the same as we do heterosexual couples?

I dreaded asking her the question: "How would you feel if I wanted to adopt a child either on my own or with a partner, forgetting for a moment my age which makes it unlikely I'd be allowed to?"

I have not been the best parent. Learning from that disaster, if in the future I met a man who had kids, with this hindsight I hope I would be able to deal with that type of situation responsibly. I would go into the relationship as a female doing her best to be a mum to her partner's children. Although folk who know my background may judge me harshly, in this designer lifestyle age we are witnessing some unusual permutations of human relationships that in my view make my situation look relatively mundane.[1]

Nowadays I wonder what would have happened had I been born a biological female and was able to have a baby when I was in my twenties or thirties, especially when I see all my girlie friends with their offspring.

I agree to disagree with Helen's view. The world is changing to the point where human beings are redefining what it is to be male and female: I believe we will always need that basic distinction in our society, yet as I discussed earlier there are individuals who are challenging the idea of gender identity itself.

Note

1 *A British man had some of his sperm frozen before having gender realignment to be a woman. He lived with his lesbian girlfriend. The couple wanted to produce a baby girl using the sperm he had frozen before his operation, and her eggs. What makes this case exceptional is that they only wanted a girl and if the fertility treatment worked the baby would have two mothers one of whom would also be her biological father. This illustrates the complexity of a particular human relationship.*

Chapter Twenty-four

I am not sure it is advisable to include Damon's thoughts on me. However, I should be up for what I hope will be some constructive criticism. That is why I agreed not to censor his version of our introduction to one another.

"When I first met Carol in 1997 she came across as domineering. If I'm honest, I think certain people feared her not because of her transgender but her outspokenness. She is the type to associate with anyone; upset her and it would be like entering a lion's cage.

Carol pursued the company of others and their dependency on her to blank out the problems she was facing. She would still express her thoughts and feelings if they were aroused by awkward questions; frequently her answers would be short, sharp and to the point. It was understood by me that she was in the process of shedding her past to be her authentic self which was difficult for her when you consider her situation. I remember incidents where Carol had angry outbursts and could be uncompromising with the person on the receiving end of them. She would willingly change roles to show her authority. It was like she had a demon inside her.

It probably reads like I'm showing her in a bad light. That, I want to underline, is not my intention. In all fairness she had a gentle side to her that only those she was close to saw and appreciated. Living in a hostel - sometimes hostile, if you'll excuse the pun - environment had caused Carol to become the centre of attention: top dog, so to speak. She demonstrated a powerful will to achieve whatever she wanted in life. Irresistibly drawn to her, she made me and others like me feel protected. We did have some bizarre people staying with us who took the sensitive ones for granted.

Much of her routine consisted of cooking, cleaning and ironing. Her popularity was huge. Residents would flock to her room daily for support and the odd drop of vino. She enjoyed her wine; in fact we all did. Our lot were beer drinkers before Carol arrived. She was regularly up for having a laugh and we would spend hours at the kitchen table or in her room drinking and smoking well into the next day.

During my nine months at the hostel, Carol settled into the role of agony aunt, although her advice could not always be taken seriously. Becoming house manager was important to her and when the job went to Colin, the daily routine shattered. From then on there probably wasn't much point in her continuing to live there. Whatever power she had was stripped from her. I moved out of the hostel. Occasional weekends she would stay with me in North Walsham. Carol was allocated a flat of her own near me. That was to change her for the better. Forming new friendships, participating in activities and projects as well as becoming part of her family again have consolidated her identity."

Damon was one of the few who sensed my frustration. From my journal it is clear how in my most depressed moments the seemingly unending wait for gender realignment nearly finished me:

"It's 16th July 2001 and I'm desperate. The ignoramuses are not letting up with their selfish behaviour, playing loud music that I'm getting in shifts, belting through the wall of my flat. I'm sitting at my computer thinking about what I've achieved since moving to Norfolk. My life is controlled by these morons who live around me. Over the last three years, on and off (largely on) I have been deprived of sleep. Earlier in this diary I mentioned how I thought everything had come to a dead stop. I've had my mum down for a couple of weeks and my world seemed to improve. I think that's because I was occupied. The minute she left I reverted to stagnation mode. Being a person who hankers for social activity and fun I'm coming to a point in my life when I should move somewhere that will allow me to grow further still.

I am kind and sensitive; unable to show these qualities properly, is it that I don't want to appear weak, or maybe I keep an emotional distance from those I really want to attract to avoid getting hurt? There's a big difference between some folk's perception of me and how I view myself. I go out of my way to look and dress right. This maleness that has held me prisoner for years doesn't want to leave."

David told me he had raised the subject of gender dysphoria with a devout Christian. How do the teachings of the Bible square with the disorder?

This Christian took the view that some media coverage suggesting gender dysphoria has a genetic origin could have generated a misguided belief: as a result, it might wrongly be thought of as a phenomenon that is caused solely by an inherited defect and because of this it is politically correct to say the gender dysphoric cannot help their way of being. Thus, it appears they are neither responsible for nor obliged to exercise the self-discipline necessary for intellectually and spiritually rising above the condition themselves to live a so-called normal life in their apparent biological gender, when from the perspective of this Christian at least, they are.

Earlier, when I recalled my stay at one of the Saint Matthew's homes in Cromer, I described two of my fellow residents, Stewart and Wayne, whose father was a Jehovah's Witness. He had been unreliably informed about me and on one of the few instances he came to visit his troubled offspring, both of whom I had befriended, he told me what he thought of me in no uncertain terms.

"You're an abomination," was all he said to me.

I may find God later. Before I can, I want time to come to terms with my recently adjusted body. Church of England bishops set out strict guidelines published in a 1991 document, 'Issues in human sexuality', that gay clergy were expected to obey. Celibacy is included in these guidelines. Imagine the torment of that when you feel natural sexual desire. I am celibate because I haven't found a person I am mutually attracted to that way whom I can trust and is able to cope with all my circumstances. Do my judges want to deny me my sexuality that is an inseparable part of my whole identity?

I now take the approach that people who discriminate against those who are different from others are the ones who need help. There wasn't a cure for seeing my real inner self as painfully at odds with the male body I had. Whatever my faults I am only another variation of nature, strange to some perhaps, but no less a rightful part of this world than anyone or anything else living here.

Chapter Twenty-five

My operation date was set for 21st February 2002. On that day, at the age of fifty-one, I was reborn.

The cost of the gender realignment surgery itself was about twelve thousand pounds. Tablets I take are not exclusively for patients suffering from gender dysphoria. Zoladex, which I have by injection, treats carcinoma of the prostate in males and endometriosis in females. For a while I took androcur. This was given to me at the Albany. It is another anticancer medicine I had received for a long period, designed for short term use. The effects of the hormones made me noticeably more feminine, increasing the size of my bust, reducing the muscle density in my arms and legs, and causing my hips to become desirably rounded. I found out that androcur contains the active ingredient cyproterone acetate. Cyproterone acetate/Ethinylestradiol is appropriated to resolve acne and female hairiness, otherwise known as hirsutism. It prevents the production and blocks the effects of testosterone. Androcur slowed down my facial hair growth making it lighter. It also stopped the possibility of my barnet falling out. Had I developed a baldness problem I would have either gone for a transplant or the Regaine solution. Through the administration of a powerful drug, the degrading hair roots can in about eighty-nine per cent of cases be rebooted into life and grow back to full strength. In other words, there is hope.

Early on in the process, the secretions of the prostate gland become less until there is no ejaculate. Lovemaking had never been easy for me, my libido so far down in my boots that when I took them off I couldn't find it. Before medication I didn't have much of a sex drive. Soon after taking it, the erections - or almost but not really ones as I used to have - dropped back to plasticine mode, then settled for permanently limp. This was a welcome development. My penis shrank to the size of what I have to admit was a rather enlarged clitoris.

Premarin, a drug also prescribed me, and that I heard was derived from pregnant mares' urine, was given to women for Hormone Replacement Therapy (HRT). My psychiatrist told me: "Take the ethinylestradiol as they are less harmful because of the reduced risk of thrombosis."

When I thought about premarin originating from mares' urine, I smiled. They extract the hormones from it, giving a whole new meaning to the phrase 'taking the piss'.

Electrolysis has to be considered by all male-to-female gender dysphorics. I was introduced to this at a place in Luton before I left Jackie in 1996, continuing to have it throughout 1997 and early 1998. For most individuals it is a painful treatment that can cost thousands of pounds; it is also time consuming and you may have to travel a long way to find an understanding practitioner. Although an important part of the male-to-female recasting, electrolysis is an aspect of gender realignment not covered by the National Health Service. It can take years to clear beard growth even at the rate of two visits per week, with costs varying between providers. Search online or pore through hard copy directories for the right salon. I have found sympathetic, caring professionals out there who realise the catastrophe gender dysphoria elicits. These practitioners may agree to perform the procedure at a reduced price. Electrolysis was vital to my positive development. The person I saw for this offered me a reasonable deal.

Now we come to the nasty little hair root itself - the commando: surviving nearly everything thrown at it, buried deep under the skin, living in its follicle, it cannot wait to stick out. You chop it off and it will grow quicker to get its own back. No matter what medication you take during transformation facial hair growth cannot be stopped once it has started. This begins at puberty. Probably the best ways for a male-to-female gender dysphoric to get rid of it are by electrolysis or laser. I found that my face began to scar due to the lengthy course of treatment I had. It should be done in stages.

Before anyone commences going through the process of having hair removed permanently it is wise to check that the electrologist involved has the relevant qualification to carry out this type of work.

Sympathising with female-to-male sufferers of gender dysphoria, the rigmarole they have to go through is more complicated and traumatic. From my male-to-female point of view the actual gender realignment surgery is usually completed in one operation. The female-to-male context is better in terms of physical appearance. Unfortunately, the surgery has to be done in stages. It includes full double mastectomy (as breasts do not disappear with hormone therapy); hysterectomy; penile, scrotal and testes construction. I heard that it is more important to confirm a diagnosis of female-to-male gender dysphoria disorder than male-to-female because rapid, irreversible changes occur when giving male hormones to women.

The female-to-male is prescribed androgens that when taken over time result in a gradual masculinisation the features of which include varying degrees of beard growth; deepening voice; change in physical appearance from softer, sinuous feminine muscular and fatty tissue distribution to solid, sinewy, masculine structures; thicker, more noticeable body hair, and, genitally, an enlarging clitoris that becomes more erectile but cannot pass as a full-fledged penis.

My operation was performed by Consultant Surgeon Mister Michael Royle at The Sussex Nuffield Hospital, Woodingdean, Brighton.

Mike Royle told me his work offered quality of life. I felt honoured because I turned out to be one of his last patients. He was planning to retire. That was sad news for the folk who would otherwise have benefited from his skill. A sense of achievement comes with the best jobs: for all the hard work he has done to meet my needs, not to mention the lives he has saved over the years through his devotion to relieving the misery of gender dysphoria, he should certainly feel that. Carol Royce wants to thank him for helping her become whole.

Labelling me mentally ill is unjust because I have tried to keep functioning on a practical level for most of my life. If any label should be attached to me it is 'selfish individual'. I deeply regret how badly I behaved. To the people unfortunate enough to enter my universe when I wasn't a nice person, thank you for putting up with me. Understandably, some will wish they had not bothered. Without them all I would have been lost. Although I was locked inside a world of contradictions that led me to behave impulsively, even aggressively towards them, my fellow-mortals gave me purpose simply by being there. If there is nowhere for you to go and, crucially, no one for you to meet, then there is no life.

I believe everyone has a purpose. Occasionally, our rationality gets blotted out by the dark side of the human condition descending on us. It is at these lowest moments we cannot, literally for the life of us, remember or do not know what our reason for being is.

I want my body donated to medical science as soon after my death as possible. Further research into gender dysphoria will hopefully lead to faster, gentler, more precise interventions, perhaps making the path to overcome it easier for individuals who are still very young, or not yet born.

Pre-op day was Wednesday 20th February 2002. On arriving at the hospital with my mum and brother I thought we might have a meal together. Disappointed that what I ended up getting was not the ploughman's lunch I asked for but a bowl of clear chicken soup - so clear there wasn't any chicken in it, more, to my palate, chicken flavour - my stay there did not start well. In the afternoon I was obliged to drink this horrible white fluid. Empty me out it did. Taking two hours to work, this stuff went through me like an attack of dysentery. One false move and there would have been a major clear up on the agenda. I imagine few folk would ever pray for constipation. I did then.

For tea chicken consommé and fruit jelly were back on the menu. The next part of the procedure was the removal of my crotch hair. This was followed by a shower to rid myself of any pubes still hanging on to my body for dear life, then a lovely, long relaxing bath. After that I had thrombo-embolus deterrent stockings fitted to control my circulation and stop me having embolisms and thromboses.

A visit from the anaesthetist and Mister Royle for a last minute chat and to sign the consent forms was a nice way to round off the day.

Ten past seven the following morning, a virtually sleepless night behind me, having had my premed I was wheeled along a hospital corridor towards a lift that took me to the operating theatre.

With the preliminaries dealt with I was put under general anaesthetic. The defunct male genitalia was removed and a vaginal pouch formed, lined with the preserved sensory nerve endings of the penis providing a quality of sensation comparable to that of a successfully functioning vagina.

To gain a few more inches of depth it is possible to have some of the bowel cut out; that would require a second operation.[1][2] Due to my age Mister Royle was not prepared to do everything in one go. Telling me I could have it performed overseas if I wanted it straight away he added that the foreign surgeons agreeing to it would almost certainly not be worried about my aftercare, whereas he would. Appreciating Mister Royle's concern, pondering this contingency I deemed it better to stick with the simpler, safer option. At least then there would be no accusations of vanity on my part, pun intended.

"Do your best," I told him, grateful that I was having the operation at all and carried out by an eminent surgeon who was concerned for my welfare. Far from being an obligatory aspect of his role in my gender realignment programme, Mister Royle visited me every twenty-four hours during my hospital convalescence, a gentleman from the old days whose kindness I will never forget.

While I was coming round, Caroline and some of the other nurses tended me, among other tasks ensuring I had not crimped any of the drainage tubes. Drifting in and out of a post-operative sleep, I knew little of what was going on. Once back in my ward I was nursed flat because if I pulled myself up I would have damaged the sutures. Intravenous fluids - which the nurses were always monitoring - continued throughout to maintain hydration. Regular checks were made on my dressings and T-bandage and antibiotics administered as required. Bed rest was forced on me, not that I could move much on that first day of freedom.

Day one, post-op, I was kept horizontal until the afternoon. A ceremonial rolling followed courtesy of the nursing staff on duty, as I understand it painfully necessary for keeping the blood flowing normally and making it easier for them to do anything else they had to. My fluid intake was increased. I had to consume huge amounts of water. A jug full with ice would be placed lovingly on my side table with the accompanying order: "I want to see this empty when I come back." Being someone who hates drinking water, having to down several glasses a day was my idea of torture. Antibiotic treatment continued, with enoxaparin given eighteen hours following the operation and then on a daily basis. Mercifully, pain killers were readily available, these the only way of keeping me sane given the degree of physical discomfort despite my high pain threshold. Being catheterised restricted my movements, to my absolute frustration, the catheter having to be kept in for a while, nurses returning at least hourly to check its status.

Medication and care plan strategies remained the same for day two. The exception was the removal of the drainage tubes once I had consumed a whole bottle of gas, taking several deep breaths before coming down from the ceiling having endured considerable discomfort.

"I thought you said this didn't hurt," I challenged a nurse. With a smile, she replied: "It depends on the patient."

Lunch consisted of consommé - again - and its usual gelatine partner. My perineal region and genitalia were examined to verify the

T-bandage was still in situ, including something like cotton wool well and truly bunged up there to cushion the surgery site.

From the point of view of treatment, day three post-op passed in a similar way to the previous. In due course a light solids diet was introduced and my vaginal pack removed personally by Mike Royle. Also around then the first dreaded uncomfortable dilatation through the large amount of tissue swelling and sutures up there was done. The plan was three sessions in a twenty-four hour period.

A week had passed since my arrival. The catheter was taken out and my urine production observed regularly. When it was confirmed I could pee and pass stools normally (I was all right with the first three legs; the fourth made my eyes water) I was given the all clear to go home.

Discharged with a letter for my doctor, I had the usual post-op survival kit for home care issued me: analgesia; KY jelly; betadine douche pack and pessaries, plus the dilatation paraphernalia that included two glass rods with a rounded taper at one end to save me from injuring myself.

At home I found it wise to stick to the recommended frequency of dilatation: primarily three times a day following surgery, changing down to twice a day at four months, once a day from one year, once or twice a week after one and a half years, and twice a month when it got to two years.

Well lubricated at the rounded tip with a combination of betadine and KY jelly, the smaller dilator is placed at the entrance to the vagina and inserted carefully, avoiding rotating or side to side movements that would damage the sutures or rupture the delicate tissue, both difficult to repair. Applying the larger dilator - the way made easier by the initial use of the smaller one - the nearer I got to the end the more unpleasant it felt, as if it could take little or no more. The griping sensation in my pelvic area came in breath-robbing spasms until I withdrew the instrument with a gentleness that any woman in a similar situation would appreciate.

Betadine gel is not necessary when using a dilator beyond the first year. Five months post surgery it was with great satisfaction that I reviewed how successful this ritual had been. Even at that stage my vagina was lubricating to some extent. This does not happen in every case.

Notes

1 Due to the male external genitalia formerly attached to me being so atrophied it was not possible to have a deeper vaginal pouch without further surgery and the potential complications of this.

2 Also known as a 'cul de sac' the vagina of the constructed female has no connecting uterus.

Chapter Twenty-six

I may have been a little slower for a while through a combination of the effects of surgery and my age but I maintained my resolve to progress. The post-operative dilatation ritual got me down. My new bits would have healed and sealed if that had not been adhered to. By late August 2002 it was only necessary to dilate once a day at night. I could have a relaxing bath then get it over and done with before retiring to bed.

What would I do with my new found freedom?: follow my desires and like some recently liberated, mature woman seek all the pleasures going to satisfy them, or help others as I had before in small ways? Had I become less judgmental? I certainly appreciated the few who did not judge me when I was vulnerable.

Lately, I am getting on with life without that inner struggle. I never expected it to be easy: it is easier because the internal conflict has gone. I had been thinking: "Does it show? Can people tell?"

When I awoke from the operation my first words were: "Am I cured?" and the nurse with me said sympathetically: "Course you are, dear."

As long as I generally pass in society and am comfortable with myself I can probably live with my worst critics telling me I am not real. Now I am rid of the useless appendage that hung between my legs. Life is to live. I can face new challenges without the distraction of gender dysphoria draining a large amount of my energy; I am able to be myself and assist those who need me.

Many years ago I looked into the possibility of raising the pitch of my voice. In those days it was hard to get this actioned through the National Health Service. I remember reading an article about a lady who had to go abroad for surgery on her voice box. She had money. Even though she also found it troublesome locating a consultant who would do it there were two surgeons prepared to carry out the procedure privately. One was in California - Beverly Hills, no less - and very expensive. The other was in Amsterdam. The second was a cheaper option; it was equally preposterous when you considered all the costs. This type of work goes under the frightening name of cricothyroid approximation. At that juncture, in America it cost the equivalent of five thousand pounds. In Holland you could have the job done for about two thousand.

I started with a male voice that was deep and gravelly. To try to correct this I had to resort to surgery. It was necessary for me to consult a specialist in the Audiology Department at Norfolk and Norwich Hospital to have an assessment and tests to find out what could be done. As I smoked and was over fifty, the speech therapist at our local clinic told me that the older I got the more difficult it would be to change the quality of the sounds coming out of my mouth. However, it was possible to save my voice. In 2002 I was still waiting to hear from the NHS about a date for an operation to modify my vocal cords.

There is a suggestion that women tend to use more frequently and emphasise emotional words while men opt for a largely cognitive approach to verbal expression. Women are also likely to show greater subtlety in the way they talk. Furthermore, the style and inflection of their speech often reveals a higher level of emotional articulacy.

Speech therapy, which focuses on raising the vocal pitch or tone, keeping the modulation from dropping too low while jointly aiming for a gentler, softer, less resonant quality to my voice, didn't work for me. Whatever improvements I made in my ten sessions each lasting an hour were lost when they finished because once separated from my therapist I all too easily reverted to a lower pitch. An hour was hard work for me because I had to think what I was saying, rendering the exercise unnatural. To this day, it is difficult for me. I won't be singing in an all-female group of choristers yet. If organisers of a mixed choir wanted bass I would be the ideal candidate: I had enough volume and depth to do it for the whole ensemble. Holding a suitable modulation was and is a challenge for me. Although in certain settings I can do it, I am called sir on the telephone. I believe it is to do with the electronic amplification through it. No matter how hard I try I cannot trick technology.

Voice modification and corrective facial surgery were the finishing touches vital for completing my picture of how I perceived myself and wished everyone else to. I didn't want anyone confused by hearing a deep voice coming from me.

The larynx or voice box belongs to the respiratory tract and is located between the pharynx and the trachea. It has walls of cartilage and muscle and contains the vocal cords which are two thick folds of mucous membrane that vibrate for speaking and singing. The cricoid and thyroid are the two main cartilages of the larynx.[1]

How masculine or feminine a voice sounds most importantly depends on its pitch and with cricothyroid approximation the cricoid and thyroid cartilages are drawn closer together to raise this.[2]

My larynx still had its basic male structure. I discussed the cricothyroid approximation agenda with my otolaryngologist, agreed with him it was necessary for me to have it done, that I was a suitable candidate for it, and that I understood the possible outcomes of the surgery, good and bad.

An important medical study that examined twenty-nine patients diagnosed with gender dysphoria provided evidence that the greater the cricothyroid distance was reduced in these persons, the more noticeable the rise in their vocal pitch.

Spiral Computed Tomography or Computed Tomography (CT) is a method of scanning the structure of the male-to-female gender dysphoric's larynx to examine its existing male framework.[3] CT has the ability to accurately determine the distance between the cricoid and thyroid cartilages affecting the vocal pitch elevation of a person both before and after surgery. Due to its high degree of accuracy, CT is a recommended method of following-up patients who have found that since treatment their vocal pitch has sadly gone back to a lower level.

Notes

1 A lump in the throat especially prominent in males is commonly known as the Adam's apple. It is part of the thyroid cartilage that forms the bulk of the front part of the larynx or voice box containing the vocal cords which it helps protect.

2 Speech pathology considerations in the management of transsexualism - a review. Oates, Jennifer M., Dacakis, Georgia., School of Communication Disorders, Lincoln Institute of Health Sciences. *British Journal of Disorders of Communication 1983. Vol.18 No.3. pp. 139–151.*

3 Spiral computed tomography before and after cricothyroid approximation, Pickuth D., Brandt S., Neumann K., Berghaus A., Spielmann R.P. and Heywang-Kobrunner, S.H. Department of Diagnostic Radiology, Martin-Luther-University, Faculty of Medicine, Halle/Saale, Germany. *Clinical Otolaryngologist 2000. 25. pp.311–314.*

Chapter Twenty-seven

If the cause of gender dysphoria is genetic and in the future possibly genomed out, think of the suffering that would prevent.[1]

Could humans' potential to develop certain illnesses be suitably removed so the resulting disabilities that restrict the lives of those suffering from them would never happen.

Suppose stem cells[2] were used successfully to reduce or cure incapacities arising from strokes, impacts, impaired motor function through diseases of the nervous system such as multiple sclerosis and Parkinson's. Imagine this treatment working for Gail, giving her back her life.

Shyness can be seen as a debility that stops a person achieving his or her potential. What if scientists could make gene therapy an effective treatment for the correction or prevention of so-called genetic weaknesses? Yet without this manipulation, some individuals might develop shyness and struggle with it, then come out the other side with qualities such as humility, self-discipline, generosity of spirit, compassion, and empathy.

Say the cause of my gender dysphoria was biologically determined. What if that had not been the case and I never fought the battle which led me to be who I am? We come back to: "Is it right to stop from happening or change what a few observers might see as handicaps, imperfections, etcetera?"

I would have been a different person because my gender dysphoria is the root of who I am now. However much it made me suffer I feel sick thinking about what might have been if I had not gone through it.

We are continuously trying to adapt to an increasingly complex world. In what I regard as their mad scramble for knowledge in order to cope with this, is the scientific community in danger of not only tampering with some of the essential qualities that make up the unique identity of any human being, but also what it is to be human? This intervening in nature is happening in other ways as well, and it is affecting our environment, that in turn affects us.

Are we playing God due to what I think is our desperate search for perfection?

I am grateful to medical science for bringing my appearance into line with my inner self. It has realigned my identity to make me a more balanced, healthier person. The medical treatment I received was necessary because it has made me happier. If I had not had my operation in 2002 I would have been no good to anyone.

Some cosmetic adjustments are imperative; others are not. Who decides what goes to the top and bottom of the list? Is this another opportunity for some of us to play God?

A few of my female friends have told me they would like some of their bits altered: larger or smaller boobs, some layers around the midriff taken away, skinnier legs, and so on. That is normal for most of the women I know.

Breast enlargement and reduction surgery are available on the NHS. While in some cases it could be argued that those who want these refinements do not really need them, in their own minds they are convinced they do. Is their cause as important as a male-to-female gender dysphoric's requirement of electrolysis to remove unwanted hair?

Botox injections to reduce sweating – one of the latest body-modification adjustments – are not available on the NHS. If you want them you have to pay for them. How essential they are depends, I suppose, on how much you sweat, and if it is a lot, the amount this is reduced.

People rely on recent advances in medicine to help them attune their minds and bodies. They want to delay the ageing process and reverse or decrease the physical and psychological discomfort of their differences from others that limit their life chances and overall happiness. Most of us, I argue, want to live as long as we can providing we have what we call quality of life.

We can think of the human life course as having roughly three stages: youth, middle-age, and old age, ending in death. Generally, going through each of these phases provides us with challenges that give our lives purpose and therefore meaning. In middle-age I have found my true identity. I am looking ahead to new possibilities of delight and fulfilment.

Hypothetically, geneticists could find a way of dramatically extending the human lifespan. How would we keep life interesting and meaningful if we were to last up to a hundred years longer than what is considered to be the norm with all the social and economic difficulties that would entail? The way we live, from the cradle to the grave, would need seriously rethinking.

Notes

1 *Chromosomes are thread-like structures that play a vital part in transmitting the characteristics we inherit from our parents. The genome is all of the heritable genetic material in the chromosomes, taken as a whole. The term genome out, which was used on a television programme, we take to mean removing particular unwanted inherited characteristics from the human genome: in other words - as we see it without any scientific knowledge in this area - an advanced form of genetic engineering.*

2 *As an embryo is forming, stem cells are life-giving cells that develop into body parts such as skin cells, blood cells, heart muscle cells, and so on. These can be stored and used later in life to treat strokes, cancer, diabetes, spinal cord injuries, Parkinson's, Hodgkin's, and Alzheimer's disease, and other illnesses and conditions.*

Chapter Twenty-eight

Our surroundings may be changing us. When trying to explain apparent contradictions in postmodern human male and female behaviour, a friend said: "Perhaps it's something in the water?" Is gender identity and sexuality influenced by strange dynamics in the uterus provoked by external factors? Could slightly higher than average levels of gender-bending chemicals found in our food, drink, environment or habitat as a whole be leading to changes in the play patterns of both male and female children? Evidence suggests a link between polychlorinated biphenyl exposure in the womb and boys being more likely to enjoy feminine play during the first seven years of their lives with girls tending to lean towards classically male associated diversions along the lines of a rough and tumble as opposed to dressing up.[1]

Some years ago a study funded by the Wellcome Trust, which is a medical charity, looked at two hundred children aged three and a half. A clear link was found between the presence of higher levels of the male hormone testosterone in a mother's womb and girls' subsequent masculine behaviour.[2]

By contrast, no link was found between mothers' testosterone levels and the later conduct of boys: researchers know these are already high in unborn males and believe that slight differences in the mother's womb would have little effect on this aspect.

Another idea the study put forward is that sexuality may be affected by testosterone levels. If, as some folk appear to surmise, the womb environment could determine that certain individuals will become homosexual is it not reasonable to offer the possibility this might also create the conditions that cause a person to eventually experience gender dysphoria?

An effusion of progesterone in the womb either from mum or the foetus I was during a critical or particularly sensitive period in the development of my brain might explain why from an early age

I felt and thought like a little girl in spite of the fact my body was besieged by male hormones. Maybe this had a lasting influence on my future gender identity and sexuality?[3]

"If you like, male-to-female gender dysphorics' equivalent of the big bang," I said to David. "On second thoughts we can do without a gender dysphoria sufferer's guide to the galaxy," I added swiftly.

What happened to my twin brother Michael then? How is it that he always wanted to be male? Maybe it is more a case of what didn't happen to him? We came from different placentas. If the hormonal anomaly only affected the placenta I was attached to could this be why eventually I felt I was trapped in the wrong sex and Michael was happy with his male gender identity?

My little boy's body didn't have the little girl's hormones to match the feeling like a little girl inside. Without ever having had naturally what other little girls have, how could I be complete for the real life test? I wasn't pretending. I can understand psychiatrists refusing surgery to people before they have tried to integrate better in society as the sex they identify with, but these cases should be receiving hormone therapy throughout the period they are living in their chosen gender. To what extent could I be a woman with a body that did not match in general anatomical and biochemical detail those of other women I knew, respected, and with whom I identified, without hormone therapy?

The fact that I and others like me had not wavered from our conviction that we are female entitled us to necessary appropriate treatment throughout the real life test.

I believe that in a room full of psychiatrists if I had said: "I feel like a woman inside," most if not all of them would have replied that didn't make me a woman as nobody knows how anybody really feels inside. Clearly I had to live like a woman to be one and be one I would.

Around June 2001 I remember reading that Professor Melissa Hines spoke of the important part the environment of the womb could play in determining the future gender role behaviour of a developing human foetus.[2]

She also pointed out that boys are socialised much more strongly to comply with what is called sex-typical behaviour than girls and this fact is illustrated by my account of growing up with my parents and male siblings in Harlow in the late 1950s and early 1960s.[2]

Although there were no girls' toys in my family home when I was young I knew that if there had been and I was caught playing with them dad would have stopped me and got the boxing gloves out immediately, taking over the back garden as an emergency rough and tumble lads only play area. There would be no girlie boys in his house or garden. Conversely, mum's friend had three girls and one boy. The girls always played with his toys without being told off for it, and my daughter Sophie by my second partner Jackie rode a bike like a boy, climbed trees, and preferred football. Sophie was Arsenal's number one fan.

Is there an increase in the number of individuals suffering from gender identity disorders?

Are females becoming more masculine and males turning into women?

From my observations there are young men around now who seem to express their masculinity in apparently more feminine ways, putting being in a steady relationship, financial security, and settling down high on their agenda.

I also see a lot of young women adopting lifestyle patterns that are perceived as traditionally masculine rather than feminine, wanting independence, to learn and develop new skills, be job creating entrepreneurs and participate in risky and exciting activities. Of course, in line with the cultural expectations of their gender, finding emotional fulfilment is still a priority.

As a general picture, the roles of women and men in our society have become blurred and in some cases reversed, the successful working woman and her male partner as spouse, housekeeper and daytime child carer being a strong example of the endmost.

I have heard that some career women are using testosterone implants which release the male sex hormone into their bloodstream, increasing their energy levels, self-confidence, self-esteem and performance in the workplace. This is so they can compete with the tougher, competitive type of male. Skin patches that also deliver the hormone into the bloodstream can apparently improve a woman's sex drive; what you might call an extreme lifestyle choice.

These days we are encouraged to be ourselves, within reason. The range of appearances and behaviours that are acceptable to many of us is increasing. This, in turn, has widened the scope of gender and sexual identity permutations in our society. Real examples of how fuzzy and indistinct the traditional male and female role boundaries have become are all around us. In fact, in the last couple of decades the frontiers of what is acceptable to many of us have been pushed back a lot further.

If there is a gradual feminisation of men and masculinisation of women surely this has serious consequences for the future? Along with sexually transmitted diseases that threaten fertility and are beginning to circumvent antibiotic treatment - as well as other causative factors reducing the ability to reproduce - there may come an age when humanity is struggling to survive.

Notes

1 *At Erasmus University in Rotterdam scientists measured levels of polychlorinated biphenyls and dioxins in the blood of 207 mothers in their final month of pregnancy. Levels of PCBs were also measured in the umbilical blood at the time of birth and in breast milk two weeks later to find out the amount each developing foetus was exposed to in the womb. The researchers asked parents to record the details of their children's play patterns up to the age of seven years.*
The behaviour described is the result of this research. It was also found that dioxins produced more feminine play in both the boys and the girls of the mothers tested. 'New gender-bending poison fear for young'. Daily Mail, Monday, October 21, 2002.

2 *See "Mothers' hormones turn girls to tomboys", by David Derbyshire, The Daily Telegraph of Monday, 4 June, 2001, which refers to the Avon Longitudinal Study of Parents and Children, led by Professor Melissa Hines.*

3 *The suggestion that a flood of progesterone in the womb could result in a male foetus becoming a little boy who from a very early age feels and thinks like a little girl is an interesting one. Similarly then, perhaps a cascade of testosterone in utero could lead to a female foetus becoming a little girl who from a very early age feels and thinks like a little boy?*

Chapter Twenty-nine

This book traces the unique life of Carol Royce. It tells a story that has serious implications for us all.

At between four and six years old a little boy began to feel and think like a little girl. From everyone else's point of view what this little boy felt and thought like was wrong: by all appearances he was a boy. Could this inner conflict have been caused by either a chromosomal irregularity[1], a freak deluge of the female hormone progesterone[2] [3] while he was still a foetus in his mother's womb - or both? Then, after he was born, he might have learned bits of feminine behaviour from his mother and other females around him, and internalised these so they became part of his growing sense of self.

He was actually she. Whichever way we look at this conundrum, there is no definite answer as to what caused Carol's gender dysphoria. Her way of being mirrors the often complex and paradoxical nature of humanity.

It appears to me that on the whole we are searching constantly for new modes of existence. Will we eventually have to redefine what it is to be human?

Before Carol and I wrote this book we had assumed that an important condition of humanness was to have a distinct gender identity. Some people though feel they are neither male nor female.

Many of us are not at peace with ourselves in the world. Even those who claim to be happy seem to need a wide range of lifestyle choices - usually only available by spending a large amount of disposable income - to be so.

Despite access to an ever greater selection of technological devices to make the daily grind easier there is a lot of sickness and marginalisation that leads to suffering. Life is becoming too sophisticated for us to cope with: we are having to develop increasingly elaborate strategies for preventing or fixing the problems it creates. In all these activities we call lifestyle choices perhaps we are really searching for a contentment we have lost.

When I think about what Carol has been through I am thankful for the love I have from my family and friends and the simple pleasure I get through my appreciation of the natural world.

I have never suffered from gender dysphoria therefore I cannot and would not want to judge Carol. Her critics told her she should have been stronger and put up with her condition. She has no interest in achieving a higher spiritual state to earn herself a place in heaven or in some long-awaited paradise on earth. She is not looking for sympathy. Her inner conflict often led her to do selfish things for which she accepts responsibility.

We hope this book presents a difficult subject as less mysterious and threatening. To try to make the concept of gender dysphoria clearer and seen as one of many variations of human beingness has been a real challenge.

It is also about life in a postmodern, technological world of accelerating activity, bringing into focus our need to consider carefully the repercussions of what is happening to the environment, and, indeed, us.

Are the globalised economy, and the self-absorbed, consumerised individual - for whom the acquisition of power, money and status appears to be the main purpose of life - dominating our culture, turning our minds away from responding naturally to our instinct to protect our species?

From Carol's and others' efforts to overcome their challenging individual differences we hold the view that human nature does exist and that its essence is an innate need for survival that in those who function adequately drives a desire for social co-operation and solidarity, justice, altruism, peace, and love.

Carol was a person struggling to adapt and survive. By suspending my judgement of her I encountered her way of being rather than a patient who had been diagnosed with gender dysphoria. I was able to experience her need to realign her body so that it was in harmony with her inner self.

David Berthelot

Notes

1 *From Carol's understanding of what she has read on the subject of gender dysphoria, at some point between conception and birth a chromosomal irregularity may occur which causes a sexual differentiation that is vague, producing visible physical changes or effects following birth or when the individual reaches sexual maturity.*

2 *We refer again to the suggestion it might be the case that before birth a hormonal surge influences the developing foetal brain possibly creating the permanent effect of an inner sex differentiation which might have happened to Carol and so many others who suffer and have suffered from gender dysphoria.*

3 *See again The Daily Telegraph of Monday, 4 June, 2001 "Mothers' hormones turn girls to tomboys", by David Derbyshire.*

Chapter Thirty

On the morning of Friday 16th May 2008 I had a haemorrhagic stroke. It was a severe bleed in my brain that further altered the course of my life. Although I recovered to a certain degree it has consequently left me with reduced mobility. I have been relying on the assistance of my friends. Being someone who wants to be in control of everything she does this new struggle has been a real setback. It should be easy having others take care of me but I cannot come to terms with the loss of a large part of my independence. I still have small aneurysms on board. Living with two bombs inside my head knowing that they could leak at any moment has made me wary. When I remember what I used to do and think about how I am now I could easily say my life is over. I am good for about an hour in the morning then it all goes downhill and I can sleep for England. The people who helped me through this were the best. I was one of the worst patients around. It took a long while to get better. Being able to leave my bed for a few minutes was an achievement. Eventually I moved from Norfolk and Norwich University Hospital to Addenbrooke's. That was followed by a period at the Centre for Specialist Rehabilitation Services where I had a lot of physiotherapy, mostly on an exercise bike, to try to get my legs working. I have since decided to do a home study correspondence course in psychology to keep my mind active and I find it fascinating. It's funny how things that don't mean much to me escape my awareness. I have to work hard to concentrate.

Through writing this book we realise how particularly complicated humans are. Having found the real me I appreciate some will never understand my story. Laid back and dangerous as ever, I laugh because that no longer matters in a world more accepting of individual differences. Clichéd, over-sentimental - whatever judgements critics throw at me - if I can help one person overcome the misery of gender dysphoria and find a true sense of self my life will have been worthwhile.

Appendix

The Gender Recognition Act 2004 became law on 4th April 2005. People who suffered from gender dysphoria can now apply to The Gender Recognition Panel that will assess their application for legal recognition in their realigned gender: if accepted, they have rights associated with this such as marrying someone of the opposite gender, forming a civil partnership with or marrying someone of the same gender, and retiring and receiving a state pension at the age agreed by law for that gender.

For years 1 had wanted to change details on my birth certificate to show that I am legally female. I was finally granted this in 2007 after receiving my gender recognition certificate.

I would like to thank Norman Lamb MP for the kindness he showed towards me in a letter I received from him on the subject of the Gender Recognition Act.

Carol Royce

Bibliography

Allen, Clifford, A textbook of psychosexual disorders, Oxford, 1986

Allgeier, Elizabeth R. and McCormick, Naomi B. Changing boundaries: Gender roles and sexual behaviour, Palo Alto: Mayfield, 1983

Archer, J. and Lloyd, B. Sex and gender, New York: Cambridge University Press, 1985

Asch, S. E. "Forming impressions of personality", *The Journal of Abnormal and Social Psychology, Vol 41(3), Jul 1946, 258–290.* doi: 10.1037/h0055756

A Working Party of the House of Bishops, Some Issues in Human Sexuality, Church House Publishing, 2003

Benjamin, Harry, The Transsexual Phenomenon, Julian Press, New York, 1966

Bonhoeffer, D. Ethics, SCM Press, 1955

Christie, Elan-Cane, The Fallacy of the Myth of Gender, Gendys Conference, USA and London, 2000

Church of England. Working Party on Human Fertilisation and Embryology, Personal Origins, Church House Publishing, 2nd revised edition, 1996

Cook, David, The moral maze, SPCK, 1983

Cossey, Caroline, My Story, Faber and Faber, 1991

Cossey, Caroline, Tula: I am a Woman, Sphere, 1982

Cowell, Roberta, Roberta Cowell's story, Heinemann, 1954

Crawley, E. The mystic rose, Spring Books, 1965

Derbyshire, David, "Mothers' hormones turn girls to tomboys", *The Daily Telegraph, Monday, 4 June, 2001.*

De Savitsch, E. Homosexuality, Transvestism, and Changes of Sex, Heinemann, 1958

Doyle, James A. The male experience, Dubuque, Iowa, William C. Brown, 1983

Fallowell, Duncan, and Ashley, April, April Ashley's odyssey, Jonathan Cape, London, 1982

Fienbloom, D. Transvestites and transsexuals, New York: Delta, 1977

Foster, Jeannette Howard, Sex variant women in literature, UK: Muller, 1958

Frazer, Sir James, The Golden Bough, London: Wordsworth, 1993

Gender Recognition Panel. "Frequently Asked Questions guidance for Gender Recognition Panel Tribunal", updated 2012, www.justice.gov.uk/tribunals/gender-recognition-panel/faqs

Goffman, Erving, Stigma. Notes on the management of spoiled identity, London: Penguin, 1963

Gooren, L.J.G. and Eklund, P. Sexual dimorphism and transsexuality, clinical observations, in **De Vries, G.J. et al (Eds):** *Progress in brain research 1984, 61, 399-406, Amsterdam, Elsevier*

Green, Richard, Sexual identity conflict in children and adults, Duckworth, 1974

Green, Richard, and Money, J. Transsexualism and sex reassignment, John Hopkins Press, USA, 1969

Gross, Alan E. "The male role and heterosexual behaviour", in *Journal of Social Issues, Winter 1978, 34(1), 87-107*

Hall, Radclyffe, The well of loneliness, Corgi, 1974

Harrington, John, Male and female identity, John Wiley & Sons, New York, 1972

Heider, Fritz, The Psychology of Interpersonal Relations, John Wiley & Sons, New York, 1958

Hodgkinson, Liz, Bodyshock: The truth about changing sex, Columbus, 1987

Houlden, J.L. Ethics and the New Testament, Continuum, 2004

Hyde, Janet S. Half the human experience: The psychology of women (3rd ed.), Lexington, Massachusetts: Heath, 1985

Hyde, Janet S. Understanding human sexuality, fourth edition, McGraw-Hill, 1990

Jay, Monica, Geraldine: For the love of a transvestite, Caliban Books, 1986

Jivaka, Lobzang, Imji Getsul: An English Buddhist in a Tibetan monastery, London: Routledge and Kegan Paul, 1962

Katchadourian, Herant A. Fundamentals of Human Sexuality, fifth edition (first published 1972), New York: Holt, Rinehart, and Winston, 1989

Katchadourian, H.A. and Lunde, D.T. Fundamentals of Human Sexuality, fourth edition, New York: Holt, Rinehart, and Winston, 1985

Keane, Dillie (mostly), Fascinating Who? Fascinating Aida: the anatomy of a group on the crest of a ripple, Elm Tree, 1986

Laub, Donald R. and Patrick Gandy (eds), Proceedings of the Second Interdisciplinary Symposium on Gender Dysphoria Syndrome, Stanford: Division of Reconstructive and Rehabilitation Surgery, Stanford Medical Center, 1973

Lloyd, Stephanie Anne and Sedgbeer, Sandra. Stephanie: A Girl in a Million, Ebury Press, 1991

Lodge, David, "Sense and Sensibility", *The Guardian, 2 November 2002.*

Lundström, Bengt, Gender dysphoria, University of Göteborg Press, 1981

Macquarrie, John, and Childress, James (eds), New dictionary of Christian ethics, SCM Press, 1990

Money, John, and Ehrhardt, Anke, Man & Woman, Boy & Girl: Gender Identity from Conception to Maturity, Northvale, N.J.: Jason Aronson, 1996

Money, John, and Tucker, Patricia, Sexual Signatures: On Being a Man or a Woman, Boston: Little, Brown & Company, 1975 (cloth); 1976 (paper)

Morris, Jan, Conundrum, New York: Harcourt Brace Jovanovich, 1974

Oates, Jennifer M., Dacakis, Georgia, "Speech pathology considerations in the management of transsexualism - a review." School of Communication Disorders, Lincoln Institute of Health Sciences. *British Journal of Disorders of Communication 1983 vol.18 no.3. pp 139–151.*

Pickuth, D., Brandt, S., Neumann, K., Berghaus, A., Spielmann, R.P. and Heywang-Kobrunner, S.H. "Spiral computed tomography before and after cricothyroid approximation", Department of Diagnostic Radiology, Martin-Luther-University, Faculty of Medicine, Halle/Saale, Germany. *Clinical Otolaryngologist 2000. 25. pp.311–314.*

Raymond, Janice, The Transsexual Empire, 1979 and 1994; reprinted by Teachers College Press, Columbia University, New York; Editions du Seuil, Paris

Scheper-Hughes, Nancy[1] and Lovell, Anne M.[2] "Breaking the circuit of social control: lessons in public psychiatry from Italy and Franco Basaglia", *Soc. Sci. Med. Vol.23. No.2, Pergamon Journals Ltd. 1986, pp.159–178.*

1 Department of Anthropology, University of California, Berkeley, CA 94720, U.S.A.

2 New York State Psychiatric Institute, 722 West 168th Street, New York, NY 10032, U.S.A.

Somerset, Georgina, A girl called Georgina, The Book Guild Limited, 1992

Stoller, R. Sex and gender, Vol I, New York: Science House, 1968

Stoller, R. The Transsexual Experiment: Sex and Gender, Vol. II, pp. 39–108, London: Hogarth Press and Institute of Psychoanalysis, 1975

Stuart, Kim, The uninvited dilemma, Metamorphosis Press, 1983

Utton, Tim, "New gender-bending poison fear for young", *The Daily Mail, Monday October 21, 2002, p.29.*

Vardy, Peter, and Grosch, Doctor Paul, The Puzzle of Ethics, Fount Paperbacks, London, 1994

Vasey, M. Strangers and friends, Hodder & Stoughton, 1995

Wålinder, Jan, Transsexualism, University of Göteborg Press, 1967

Whittle, Stephen and Turner, Lewis, "'Sex Changes'? Paradigm Shifts in 'Sex' and 'Gender' Following the Gender Recognition Act?", *Manchester Metropolitan University, Sociological Research Online, Volume 12, Issue 1.* <http://www.socresonline.org.uk/12/1/whittle.html> doi: 10.5153/sro.1511 Published: 31 Jan 2007

Wilson, Colin, "Are some people born criminal?" *The Daily Mail, Friday 2nd August, 2002.*

Wilson, Glenn, (ed.), Variant Sexuality: Research and Theory, Croom Helm, London and Sydney, 1987

Woodhouse, Annie, Fantastic women: sex, gender and transvestism, Macmillan Education, London, 1989

www.ingramcontent.com/pod-product-compliance
Lightning Source LLC
Chambersburg PA
CBHW020517100426
42813CB00030B/3283/J